THE

OXFORD

BOOK OF

AUSTRALIAN

WOMEN'S EDITED BY SUSAN LEVER

VERSE

Melbourne
OXFORD UNIVERSITY PRESS
Oxford Auckland New York

OXFORD UNIVERSITY PRESS AUSTRALIA

Oxford New York
Athens Auckland Bangkok Bombay
Calcutta Cape Town Dar es Salaam Delhi
Florence Hong Kong Istanbul Karachi
Kuala Lumpur Madras Madrid Melbourne
Mexico City Nairobi Paris Singapore
Taipei Tokyo Toronto
and associated companies in
Berlin Ibadan

OXFORD is a trade mark of Oxford University Press

National Library of Australia
Cataloguing-in-Publication data:

The Oxford book of Australian women's verse.

Includes index.
ISBN 0 19 553505 7.

1. Australian poetry—Women authors. I. Lever, Susan, 1950-   .
II. Title: Australian women's verse. III. Title.

A821.00809287

This project has been assisted by the Commonwealth Government
through the Australia Council, its arts funding and advisory body.

Cover design by Guy Mirabella
Typeset by Solo Typesetting, South Australia
Printed by Australian Print Group
Published by Oxford University Press,
253 Normanby Road, South Melbourne, Australia

CONTENTS

INTRODUCTION

Twenty years ago Kate Jennings collected a book of Australian women's poetry, which claimed a hearing for feminist voices in the predominantly male world of poetry publishing and criticism of the time. As its title indicated, *Mother I'm Rooted* proposed a radical poetry for feminist ideals, and much of the poetry in it reflects the energy and experimentation of the 1970s. In 1986 Susan Hampton and Kate Llewellyn edited the *Penguin Book of Australian Women Poets*, which recorded the growth in awareness of Australian women poets that had occurred in the previous decade. This *Oxford Book of Australian Women's Verse* marks a further stage in the recognition of Australian women's poetry, which has now become a focus of mainstream interest and study. So many Australian women poets have been publishing and receiving critical attention in the past ten years that they can no longer be considered marginalised.

The time has come, therefore, for an anthology that presents the historical record of Australian women's poetry publishing, and that enables readers to see recent women's poetry in the context of women's writing since white settlement. The second-wave feminists of the 1970s often assumed that they were the first generation of women to speak out. Indeed, there seemed to be no spare time or energy available to allow feminists to retrieve the history of past generations of women. Now, with women poets commanding a fairer share of public attention, it is possible to reflect on past achievements of women writers and to see that their poetry offers not so much a single 'women's tradition', but a range of attitudes and formal styles.

This collection includes poetry published in English and written by women born or living in Australia, spanning the period from 1838 (the publication date of Eliza Hamilton Dunlop's poem) to the present. While it has the aim of all good anthologies—to publish poetry that the editor believes will delight readers—it also tries to present the full range of women's poetry and illustrate the changes in literary taste that make different styles flourish or disappear in each generation. The verse is arranged here by poet's birthdate rather than in order of publication. Nevertheless, reading the collection through from beginning to end gives some indication of the broad changes that have taken place in Australia. In particular, it reveals the ways in which new influences emerge in verse styles.

Contrary to widespread belief, at every stage in Australia's history women poets have been published and respected by their contemporaries. Research for this collection revealed that almost every impressive poem published in magazines and journals during the late nineteenth century and early twentieth century eventually found its way into a book. This kind of recognition, however, rarely extended beyond poets' lifetimes, as changes in poetic fashions meant that their work seemed outdated to new generations.

The literary historians and anthologists who uphold the reputations of the past usually seek some universal qualities in poetry; they look for poetry that transcends both its time and its audience. In fact, however, most poetry belongs very much to its own time and culture, and readers of the poetry of the past must respond not only to the individual imagination of the poet, but also to some of the cultural context in which the poetry was written. The elements of context and audience are particularly important in reading poetry by women, because it is here that the art of women most differs from that of men.

When arguments about the inherent differences between the sexes turn to poetry, a number of contradictory positions may be taken. Some critics claim that women's poetry is 'obedient' to current literary fashions; others that it has been overlooked because it refuses to conform to the dominant order prescribed by men. Theories about the sex-determined nature of poetry usually come to ground on the differences between poetry by individual women, since these are often greater than the proposed disparities between the poetry of men and women as a whole. Some readers and writers (including some women poets) see the argument about differences as irrelevant—arguing that there is poetry, and the sex of its author bears no relationship to whether it is good poetry or not. Yet Australian men and women have lived different kinds of lives in accord with prevailing notions of 'appropriate' behaviour and, as a result, poetry has played different roles in their lives. This cultural difference means that women's poetry has been written out of different life conditions, and sometimes addresses different audiences, from that of men. For example, women have often written poetry that expresses community experiences, rather than the more individualistic reflections associated with high poetry. Poems here by Fidelia Hill, Dorothy Drain and Oodgeroo address the particular communities that each perceived as audience—whether that be the white pioneers of Hill, Drain's suburban housewives, or Oodgeroo's Aboriginal Australians and complacent whites. Most Australian women poets have also written verse for children; however, such verse seemed inappropriate for this collection's adult audience, and readers will need to seek the verse of poets such as Ruth Bedford, Lydia Pender and Annie Rentoul in children's anthologies.

As this anthology shows, the place of poetry in women's lives has changed with the passing of time, and women from different backgrounds have responded to different aspects of poetry. So the body of poetry written by women has been remarkably varied, in contrast to the monotone proposed by some critics. In selecting poems I have tried to provide readers with some sense of the variety of women's interests and writing. It would have been possible to choose only poems written about the status of women, or about domestic life, or poems in the patriotic vein of Dorothea Mackellar's 'My Country'. While recent anthologies of war verse suggest that women rarely considered the dangers and difficulties of war, I could have collected a book full of such pieces, many of them, such as Ethel Anderson's 'Squatter's Luck', celebrating the bravery of Australian men. I have also tried to include the best poems to represent each poet, though such choice must of course be subjective. Preference has been given to poems that show some command over their chosen genre and that express their insights in a vivid language. In the case of poets such as Judith Wright, Gwen Harwood and Rosemary Dobson, whose entire body of writing might be included in 'best', I have selected a range of poetry, including some early and some recent work. Fortunately, selected editions of the work of these poets are currently available to satisfy readers' appetites for more.

Looking back on the poetry of the nineteenth century, one can see how the English High Romantic tradition has dominated literary history, overwhelming the presence of other traditions practised in the period. This Romantic tradition and the pressure it placed on poets to accommodate the Australian landscape within their European heritage can be seen in the poetry of 'Australie' and Catherine Martin, and in Caroline Carleton's 'Wild Flowers of Australia', her answer to Adam Lindsay Gordon's misrepresentation of Australia as the land 'where bright blossoms are scentless and songless bright birds' ('A Dedication'). Ada Cambridge, Mary Fullerton, and Mary Gilmore in some modes, demonstrate other more direct and consciously simple styles. Their distillations of wisdom or logical meditations represent a kind of poetry that has fallen so far from favour in post-imagistic times that it may be difficult to appreciate their achievements. Ironically, this is not because they present any difficulties in comprehension, but because we have learned to value the complex concrete image over the abstract statement, the particular insight over the general observation.

A lower branch of the Romantic tradition reaches out in the popular ballad and vernacular verse forms that Robbie Burns made part of the heritage of immigrants of both English and Celtic backgrounds. Mary Hannay Foott's 'Where the Pelican Builds' gained immense popularity from the time of its first publication in the 1880s, but other excellent examples of the Australian ballad tradition can be found here in Louisa Lawson's 'A Pound a Mile' and Marie Pitt's 'Clan Call', along with contemporary variations in the songs of Glen Tomasetti and Judy Small. While the egalitarian enthusiasms of the 1890s may explain the attention to vernacular speech in Sydney Partrige's 'Sund'y', such attempts to mimic the voices of ordinary people are apparent from Louisa Lawson's verse, to the work of contemporary performance poets such as Joanne Burns and Ania Walwicz. Sometimes these voices represent a political claim on poetry by those who feel excluded from the 'educated' voice of high poetry.

For educated poets in the early twentieth century, the European classical heritage provided a means of acting out possibilities outside the rather puritanical standards of Australian life. Zora Cross was able to write erotic love sonnets within the frame of Shakespearean and classical allusion; Dulcie Deamer could explore female desire by dramatising the thoughts of Messalina or a young Christian martyr in Rome. Up to about 1930, fairies, goblins and witches also allowed women poets to play with ideas foreign to the often mundane ideals of Australian life. Very few of these creatures appear here, but Mabel Forrest's 'Kassaptu (the Assyrian Witch)' provides a glimpse of their exotic possibilities in the hands of a gifted poet.

After the 1930s there appears to have been a distinct change in the tenor of women's verse, perhaps a sign that the 'Celtic Twilight' fashion had run its course, and modernism had begun to impinge on even the farthest reaches of English-writing culture. Of all the poets mentioned in Australian women's poetry, W. B. Yeats is honoured most often, and this change may follow Yeats's own remarkable development into a modernist. By the 1940s a new kind of nature poetry had emerged, sometimes influenced by Jindyworobak ideas about finding an indigenous poetic tradition. It is this kind of poetry that established Judith Wright's early reputation and can be found here in poetry by Nancy Cato and Mary Finnin.

One of the difficulties of arranging the poetry by author's date of birth has been the lack of indication this gives of the place of any one poem within the career of the poet, and interested readers should check the publishing information in the acknowledgments list at the back of the book. Chronology based on authors' dates means that Mary Finnin's poetry of the 1950s is closely followed by Elizabeth Riddell's poems published in the 1980s; Nan McDonald's 1960s pieces come after quite recent poems by Gwen Harwood; and Nancy Cato's poems, all published before 1951, come after Barbara Giles's and Vera Newsom's 1980s and 1990s poems. What does become apparent from this are the late-life publishing careers of Riddell, Giles and Newsom—perhaps an older generation of women have benefited from the activities of younger poets. Indeed, the achievements of the women born between 1915 and 1925 seem quite astonishing from this perspective.

This said, the inspirational place of Judith Wright in the history of Australian women's poetry since the Second World War needs to be acknowledged. Wright emerged with a talented generation of men poets, including A. D. Hope, James McAuley, Douglas Stewart and David Campbell. She not only held her place among these poets, but has continued to write poetry that challenges current literary and social values. Wright is not simply a poet of the Hope, McAuley and Stewart generation, she has become a poet of each of the generations since, adapting and refining her technique while maintaining a clear vision of the place of poetry in society. For younger women poets—and for those her own age—Wright has shown the possibilities for poetry as a means of combining complex art with passionate private and public concerns.

Wright read the poems of Oodgeroo (then Kath Walker) when they came in manuscript form to the Jacaranda Press in 1963, and subsequently took an active part in promoting her work. In poems such as 'Dawn Wail for the Dead' and 'No More Boomerang' Oodgeroo adapted popular poetic forms to political purposes. While some readers at first found her work naive, by a shrewd use of familiar forms Oodgeroo managed to gain a wide audience for her poetry and, at the same time, to raise awareness of Aboriginal experience among the white community. In 'Last of His Tribe' Oodgeroo is quite consciously recasting the traditional viewpoint of white poetry to address the immediate problems of her people. Her success paved the way for younger Aboriginal poets and activists, such as Kevin Gilbert and Lionel Fogarty, as well as the other Aboriginal women represented here—Daisy Utemorrah, Bobbi Sykes and Charmaine Papertalk-Green.

Aboriginal verse in translation has not been included in this collection, because the act of translation necessarily converts a non-Western tradition into an approximation of one. (There is no other verse in translation represented in the anthology.) Nineteenth-century Aboriginal life can only be glimpsed here through some white poets' encounters with it, rather than through white translations of tribal songs. Eliza Hamilton Dunlop's 'The Aboriginal Mother', first published a few days before the execution of the men convicted for the massacre of Aborigines at Myall Creek, frames its indictment of white brutality in terms of a surviving woman's lullaby to her child. Honora Frances Kelly's '"King Jimmy" (Colonial Idyll of the King)', in which a benign white voice patronises the last member of a tribe, reduced to the 'poor harmless son of Austral's clime', describes a later phase of black/white relations. A generation later, Mary Gilmore began experimenting with Aboriginal verse forms and metaphors, and 'The Hunter of the Black' brings a bleak irony to her account of white murderousness. These poems show the ways in which white poets tried to adapt what they knew of Aboriginal poetic traditions to their own inherited traditions. These attempts can also be seen in some of Nancy Cato's and Judith Wright's poetry.

No matter how sympathetic, the white poets who attempted to explore the Aboriginal experience could only guess at Aboriginal responses; Oodgeroo claimed a voice for her own community, and she adapted both Aboriginal and English poetic traditions to popular purposes. Her humour, perhaps, most marks the difference between her poetry and that of the generations of white women who had earnestly mimicked the Aboriginal voice. Contemporary poets, such as Bobbi Sykes and Charmaine Papertalk-Green, have continued the Aboriginal poetic tradition of political awareness and wit initiated by Oodgeroo.

Just as Aboriginal women's reclaiming of themselves as poetic subjects can be seen in this anthology, the influence of European rather than English and Celtic forms can be seen in poetry published since the Second World War. Margaret Diesendorf, Fay Zwicky and Antigone Kefala, for example, write poetry that not only deals with European subjects, but conveys some of the emotional atmosphere, and the searching beneath the surfaces, of contemporary European poetry. By comparison, English- and Celtic-influenced poetry appears quite hearty and extroverted. In general, Australian women's poetry, even when most influenced by modernism, tends to address the social world rather than explore the psychological state of the individual.

The Asian immigration to Australia has not yet begun to show its full impact on Australian poetry, but it seems probable that the great traditions of Indian, Chinese, Japanese and Southeast Asian poetry will increasingly influence Australian-born poets. In Helen Haenke's 'Pear Tree' and Rosemary Dobson's 'The Three Fates' we find references to classical Chinese poetry and its ideal of contemplative simplicity. Other poets make reference to the epic narrative poetry of India, and Dipti Savaranamuttu's poetry confronts the cultural divide between East and West. Asia, of course, does not represent a single culture and these two strands—transcendent lyric simplicity and culturally specific storytelling—will undoubtedly be joined by others as Chinese- and Vietnamese-born poets begin to publish.

Since the 1970s more and more Australian women have turned to poetry as the appropriate form to explore the traditional subjects of love, the landscape, and the celebration of sensual perception, as well as to express their responses to the social world. A corresponding growth in poetry publishing has made it difficult to select recent poems for such a broad and historically based anthology. Essentially, the choice fell between the representation of as many poets as possible by a single poem each, or an attempt to indicate the range of poetry by choosing several poems from poets who seem to represent certain styles. I have chosen the second approach. This means that the burst of energy of the early 1970s is represented mainly by Vicki Viidikas, Susan Hampton, Joanne Burns and Pamela Brown.

The spirit of experiment has continued in the work of Gig Ryan, J. S. Harry and Dorothy Porter, alongside more traditional poetry by writers such as Jean Kent, Diane Fahey and Rhyll McMaster. Some recent poetry, particularly that of Ania Walwicz and Joanne Burns, needs to be recited for full effect and probably works best when performed by the poets, but I have selected poems that seem accessible on the page as well.

While this collection attempts to represent the range of contemporary women's poetry, I have also taken the anthologist's prerogative in choosing poets that I think deserve particular attention. Sometimes these are not the poets best known in literary circles. We can only speculate about the reputations of these poets in the future, but I have tried to maintain the long view that was possible in selecting the nineteenth-century material. I would like to think that some of my contemporary choices will be considered worthy of inclusion in anthologies compiled in fifty years' time.

This anthology, of course, can merely provide a sketch of the nature of women's verse writing as a whole over more than 150 years. The selection does not include, for example, epic verse such as Catherine Martin's 'The Explorers', nor 'Australie's' ambitious verse play 'The Emigrants'. Menie Parkes's 'Our Darling's Lover' is but a sample of the mass of nineteenth-century poetry about youthful death that rested on a kind of morbid eroticism. Dorothy Drain's weekly contributions to the *Australian Women's Weekly* over some twenty-five years are reduced here to one example, and there is sparse representation of the popular and children's verse that was the major contribution of many Australian women writers. Despite such exclusions, I hope readers, whether men or women, Australians or not, will find much here to enjoy.

Marie Louise Ayres helped me to prepare the anthology by working through bibliographies, sifting poems, researching biographies and arguing with the final selection. A grant from the University College, Australian Defence Force Academy, made her help possible. Geoff Page generously offered advice on contemporary selections, though the final choices are my sole responsibility. I also thank several friends, including my daughters, who read and discussed poetry with me.

Susan Lever
Canberra 1995

Fidelia Hill

Recollections

Yes, South Australia! three years have elapsed
Of dreary banishment, since I became
In thee a sojourner; nor can I choose
But sometimes think on thee; and tho' thou art
A fertile source of unavailing woe,
Thou dost awaken deepest interest still.—
Our voyage past, we anchor'd in that port
Of our New Colony, styled Holdfast Bay:
In part surrounded by the range sublime
Of mountains, with Mount Lofty in their centre:—
Beautiful mountains, which at even-tide
I oft have gazed upon with raptur'd sense,
Watching their rose-light hues, as fleeting fast
Like fairy shadows o'er their verdant sides
They mock'd the painter's art, and to pourtray
Defied the utmost reach of poet's skill!—
The new year open'd on a novel scene,—
New cares, new expectations, a new land!—
Then toil was cheer'd, and labour render'd light,
Privations welcom'd, every hardship brav'd,
In the blest anticipation of reward:—
(Which some indeed deserv'd, but ne'er obtain'd)
Some who unceasingly, had lent their aid,
And time, and information, to promote
The interests of the rising Colony—
Still flattering hope on the dark future smil'd,
Gilding each object with fallacious dyes,
And picturing pleasure, that *was not to be!*
They bore me to the future Capitol,
Ere yet 'twas more than desart—a few tents,
Scatter'd at intervals, 'mid forest trees,
Marked the abode of men. 'Twas a wide waste,
But beauteous in its wildness.—Park-like scenery
Burst on the astonish'd sight; for it did seem
As tho' the hand of art, had nature aided,
Where the broad level walks—and verdant lawns,
And vistas grac'd that splendid wilderness!
'Twas then they hail'd me as the *first* white lady
That ever yet had enter'd Adelaide.—
Can time e'er teach me to forget the sound,

Or gratulations that assail'd me then,
And cheer'd me at the moment, or efface
The welcome bland of the distinguish'd one—
Who fix'd the site, and form'd the extensive plan
Of that young City?—He hath pass'd away
To the dark cheerless chambers of the tomb!
But Adelaide if crown'd with fortune, shall
To after age perpetuate his name!—

•

One tent was pitch'd upon the sloping bank
Of the stream Torrens, in whose lucid wave
Dipp'd flow'ring shrubs—the sweet mimosa there
Wav'd its rich blossoms to the perfum'd breeze,
High o'er our heads—amid the stately boughs
Of the tall gum tree—birds of brightest hues
Or built their nests, or tun'd 'their wood-notes wild,'
Reposing on the rushes, fresh and cool,
Which a lov'd hand had for my comfort strew'd:—
This, this methought shall be my happy home!
Here may I dwell, and by experience prove,
That tents with love, yield more substantial bliss
Than Palaces without it, can bestow.

FINIS

Eliza Hamilton Dunlop

The Aboriginal Mother

(from Myall's Creek)

Oh! hush thee—hush my baby,
   I may not tend thee yet.
Our forest-home is distant far,
   And midnight's star is set.
Now, hush thee—or the pale-faced men
   Will hear thy piercing wail,
And what would then thy mother's tears
   Or feeble strength avail!

Oh, could'st thy little bosom,
  That mother's torture feel,
Or could'st thou know thy father lies
  Struck down by English steel;
Thy tender form would wither,
  Like the *kniven* in the sand,
And the spirit of my perished tribe
  Would vanish from our land.

For thy young life, my precious,
  I fly the field of blood,
Else had I, for my chieftan's sake,
  Defied them where they stood;
But basely bound my woman's arm,
  No weapon might it wield:
I could but cling round him I loved,
  To make my heart a shield.

I saw my firstborn treasure
  Lie headless at my feet,
The goro on this hapless breast,
  In his life-stream is wet!
And thou! I snatched thee from their sword,
  It harmless pass'd by thee!
But clave the binding cords—and gave,
  Haply, the power to flee.

To flee! my babe—but wither?
  Without my friend—my guide?
The blood that was our strength is shed!
  He is not by my side!
Thy sire! oh! never, never
  Shall *Toon Bakra* hear our cry:
My bold and stately mountain-bird!
  I thought not he could die.

Now who will teach thee, dearest,
  To poise the shield, and spear,
To wield the *koopin*, or to throw
  The *boommerring*, void of fear;
To breast the river in its might;
  The mountain tracks to tread?
The echoes of my homeless heart
  Reply—the dead, the dead!

And ever must the murmur
  Like an ocean torrent flow:
The parted voice comes never back,
  To cheer our lonely woe:
Even in the region of our tribe,
  Beside our summer streams,
'Tis but a hollow symphony—
  In the shadow-land of dreams.

Oh hush thee, dear—for weary
  And faint I bear thee on—
His name is on thy gentle lips,
  My child, my child, *he's gone!*
Gone o'er the golden fields that lie
  Beyond the rolling clouds,
To bring thy people's murder cry
  Before the Christian's God.

Yes! o'er the stars that guide us,
  He brings my slaughter'd boy:
To shew their God how treacherously
  The stranger men destroy;
To tell how hands in friendship pledged
  Piled high the fatal pire;
To tell, to tell of the gloomy ridge!
  and the *stockmen's human fire*.

Caroline Carleton

The Song of Australia

There is a land where summer skies
Are gleaming with a thousand dyes,
Blending in witching harmonies;
And grassy knoll and forest height
Are flushing in the rosy light,
And all above is azure bright—
                    Australia!

There is a land where honey flows,
Where laughing corn luxuriant grows,
Land of the myrtle and the rose;
On hill and plain the clust'ring vine
Is gushing out with purple wine,
And cups are quaffed to thee and thine—
                    Australia!

There is a land where treasures shine
Deep in the dark unfathom'd mine
For worshippers at Mammon's shrine;
Where gold lies hid, and rubies gleam,
And fabled wealth no more doth seem
The idle fancy of a dream—
                    Australia!

There is a land where homesteads peep
From sunny plain and woodland steep,
And love and joy bright vigils keep;
Where the glad voice of childish glee
Is mingling with the melody
Of nature's hidden minstrelsy—
                    Australia!

There is a land where floating free
From mountain top to girdling sea
A proud flag waves exultingly!
And Freedom's sons the banner bear,
No shackl'd slave can breathe the air,
Fairest of Britain's daughters fair—
                    Australia!

Wild Flowers of Australia

Oh say not that no perfume dwells;
  The wilding flowers among,
Say not that in the forest dells
  Is heard no voice of song.

The air is laden with the scent
  Borne from the clustering flower,
With which the wattle is besprent;
  Like Danae's golden shower.

And silv'ry wattles bending low,
   Sweet incense scatter far—
When night-winds kiss the pensile bough,
   Beneath the evening star.

And there are flowers of varying dye;
   Now white, now blushing red,
Their beauteous blossoms charm the eye,
   And fragrant odours shed.

There's perfume breath'd from Austral flowers,—
   And melody is there
Not such as in far Albion's bowers
   Falls on th' accustom'd ear.

But thrilling snatches of wild song,
   Pour'd forth from lonely glen—
Where winds the hidden creek along
   Far from the haunts of men.

And hoarser notes in wild woods heard
   Sound like strange harmonies,
As flashes past the bright-winged bird
   Gleaming in azure skies.

Then say not that no perfume dwells,
   The wilding flowers among;
Say not that in the forest dells
   Is heard no voice of song!

Caroline Leakey

The Prisoners' Hospital,
Van Diemen's Land

O prison-house of sighing!
   Where the weary and the worn,
The long-pent and the dying,
   Lie friendless and forlorn;
Where sickness preys on weariness,
   And prey they both on life;
The mother weeps in dreariness,
   And pines the lonely wife.

Where tender babe and wasted child
   Look eagerly around,
And wonder why the face that smiled,
   Can nowhere *now* be found.
Where on the sickly little one
   Rests no kind eye of love;
Its pleading moan there heark'neth none,
   Save God, who dwells above.

Meet old and young together,
   Each their numbered days to fill;
One grudging still the other,
   And all fretting at God's will.
The widow mourns her widowhood,
   All childless and alone;
The old man dies in solitude,
   None near to call his own.

The piercing shriek of madness,
   And the hollow face of care,
Meet tears and sighs of sadness,
   And the wailings of despair.
Where the captive exile hasteth,
   And striveth to be free,
For the bitterness he tasteth
   Of sin's deep misery.

The restless cry for morning,
   The weary pine for night,
But darkness nor the dawning
   Cometh e'er to them aright.
Where time, so heavy dragg'd with strife,
   On wheels of grief moves slow;
Bearing the wretched on through life,
   Up paths of human woe.

O'er the dead there is no weeping,
   By the dying none to pray,
That Death's dark shade o'er creeping,
   Be illumined by Love's ray.
But cold, they watch each other die,
   Still shuddering to see
Yon ruthless hand close up each eye,
   As theirs must closèd be.

Oh! ere Death's heavy bolt be drawn
    Upon life's gate for ever,
And deeps of black perdition yawn
    Beneath their souls for ever,
Thou who sweet mercy lov'st to show,
    Look down! forgive—relent!
Haste, Lord, ere sealèd this worst woe,
    On earth's long banishment.

Menie Parkes

Our Darling's Lover

Death fell in love with our darling fair,
With blue bright eyes and shining hair,
And pulpy lips of unkissed bloom,
And brows made stern with young thought's gloom.

He lifted the veil from his sacred face,
He showed her his form of matchless grace;
And our darling told us, with fluttering breath,
She had plighted her troth to the Angel Death.

Her hair grew lank from his damp caress,
And her brow was cold where his lips did press;
And the child of our hearts was lost, we knew,
For Death is a lover, fond, firm, and true.

Her voice was clear and toned with glee,
And her eye was bright and her step was free;
Her pearly cheek he painted with light,
She bloomed to an angel before our sight.

There came to us soon the parting day,
And our darling went with a smile away;
With a beaming smile and a panting breath,
She sprang to the arms of her lover, Death.

But the grief was ours who were left behind,
With our tearful eyes all bleared and blind;
And still the sighs catch our baffled breath
For our darling, loved by the Angel—Death.

Ada Cambridge

The Physical Conscience

The moral conscience—court of last appeal—
   Our word of God—our Heaven-sent light and guide—
   From what high aims it lures our steps aside!
To what immoral deeds it sets its seal!
That beacon lamp has lost its sacred fire;
   That pilot-guide, compelling wind and wave,
   By slow, blind process, has become the slave
Of all-compelling custom and desire.

Not so the conscience of the body. This,
   Untamed and true, still speaks in voice and face,
In cold lips stiffened to the loveless kiss,
   In shamed limbs shrinking from unloved embrace,
In love-born passion, that no laws compel,
Nor gold can purchase, nor ambition sell.

A Wife's Protest

1
Like a white snowdrop in the spring
   From child to girl I grew,
And thought no thought, and heard no word
   That was not pure and true.

2
And when I came to seventeen,
   And life was fair and free,
A suitor, by my father's leave,
   Was brought one day to me.

3
'Make me the happiest man on earth,'
   He whispered soft and low.
My mother told me it was right
   I was too young to know.

4

And then they twined my bridal wreath
   And placed it on my brow.
It seems like fifty years ago—
   And I am twenty now.

5

My star, that barely rose, is set;
   My day of hope is done—
My woman's life of love and joy—
   Ere it has scarce begun.

6

Hourly I die—I do not live—
   Though still so young and strong.
No dumb brute from his brother brutes
   Endures such wanton wrong.

7

A smouldering shame consumes me now—
   It poisons all my peace;
An inward torment of reproach
   That never more will cease.

8

O how my spirit shrinks and sinks
   Ere yet the light is gone!
What creeping terrors chill my blood
   As each black night draws on!

9

I lay me down upon my bed,
   A prisoner on the rack,
And suffer dumbly, as I must,
   Till the kind day comes back.

10

Listening from heavy hour to hour
   To hear the church-clock toll—
A guiltless prostitute in flesh,
   A murderess in soul.

11

Those church-bells chimed the marriage chimes
   When he was wed to me,
And they must knell a funeral knell
   Ere I again am free.

12

I did not hate him then; in faith
  I vowed the vow 'I will;'
Were I his mate, and not his slave,
  I could perform it still.

13

But, crushed in these relentless bonds
  I blindly helped to tie,
With one way only for escape,
  I pray that he may die.

14

O to possess myself once more,
  Myself so stained and maimed!
O to make pure these shuddering limbs
  That loveless lust has shamed!

15

But beauty cannot be restored
  Where such a blight has been,
And all the rivers in the world
  Can never wash me clean.

16

I go to church; I go to court;
  No breath of scandal flaws
The lustre of my fair repute;
  For I obey the laws.

17

My ragged sister of the street,
  Marked for the world's disgrace,
Scarce dares to lift her sinful eyes
  To the great lady's face.

18

She hides in shadows as I pass—
  On me the sunbeams shine;
Yet, in the sight of God, her stain
  May be less black than mine.

19

Maybe she gave her all for love,
  And did not count the cost;
If so, her crown of womanhood
  Was not ignobly lost.

20

Maybe she wears those wretched rags,
  And starves from door to door,
To keep her body for her own
  Since it may love no more.

21

If so, in spite of church and law,
  She is more pure than I;
The latchet of those broken shoes
  I am not fit to tie.

22

That hungry baby at her breast—
  Sign of her fallen state—
Nature, who would but mock at mine,
  Has made legitimate.

23

Poor little 'love-child'—spurned and scorned,
  Whom church and law disown,
Thou hadst thy birthright when the seed
  Of thy small life was sown.

24

O Nature, give no child to me,
  Whom Love must ne'er embrace!
Thou knowest I could not bear to look
  On its reproachful face.

London

The gorgeous stream of England's wealth goes by,
  Mixed with the mud and refuse, as of old—
  The hungry, homeless, naked, sick and cold;
Want mocked by waste and greedy luxury.
There, in their downy carriage-cushions, lie
  Proud women whose fair bodies have been sold
  And bought for coronet or merchant gold—
For whose base splendours envious maidens sigh.

Some day the social ban will fall on them—
   On wanton rich who taunt their starving kin;
Some day the social judgment will condemn
   These 'wedded harlots' in their shame and sin.
A juster world shall separate them then
From all pure women and all honoured men.

Ordained

1

Through jewelled windows in the walls
   The tempered daylight smiles,
And solemn music swells and falls
   Adown these stately aisles;
Beneath that carven chancel-rood
Low murmurs, hushed to silence, brood;
   One voice on prayer appeals
For Holy Spirit's quickening grace
To light his now anointed face
   Who at the altar kneels.

2

One hour ago, like us, he trod
   Along these cloisters dim—
Now we are bid to reverence God
   Made manifest in him;
To mock at our enlightened sense
And dearly won experience,
   So far beyond his own;
To take him for our heaven-sent guide
Upon these seas, so wild and wide,
   To him as yet unknown.

3

Unconscious of the coming strife,
   Unformed in mind and thought,
Without one ripe idea of life
   Save what his school books taught,
An ignorant boy, he vows a vow
To think and feel as he does now
   Till his gold locks are grey;
Pledges his word to learn no more—
To add no wisdom to the store
   His young mind holds to-day.

4

How shall he keep this senseless oath
   When once a full-grown man?
How shall he check his upward growth
   To fit this meagre plan?
Only by ruthless pinching out
Of all the fairest shoots that sprout,
   As on a healthy tree,
From his expanding brain and heart—
Defrauding his diviner part
   Of its virility.

5

And thus shall youthful passion pale
   In native force and fire;
And thus shall soaring pinions fail,
   Bedraggled in the mire;
This tender conscience, now so bright,
Lose its fine sense of wrong and right—
   Dulled with a moral rust;
This ardent intellect be damped,
This eager spirit starved and cramped—
   Choked in mediaeval dust.

6

Thus shall the fettered arm grow numb,
   And blind the bandaged eye;
Thus shall the silenced voice grow dumb,
   As year by year goes by;
Until at last, from long abuse
And lack of free and wholesome use,
   All manhood's powers decline;
And, like a lamp unfed, untrimmed,
Intelligence, once bright, is dimmed,
   No more to burn and shine.

7

Then may we see this sanguine youth—
   Born for a nobler lot—
Turn traitor to the highest truth
   Because he knows it not;
Serving for Mammon, veiled as God,
Cringing for high-born patron's nod,
   For social place and gain,
While he mechanically yields
The produce of his fallow fields—
   Husks of long-garnered grain.

8

No more a brave and honest man,
   Whose conscience is his own,
But worse than thief and courtesan
   To degradation grown;
A cheat and hypocrite, content,
In shelter of base precedent,
   The downward path to tread,
Lest he should lose his Esau's bowl,
That bought the birthright of his soul,
   And have to earn his bread.

9

Or, if remorsefully aware
   Of his ignoble case,
Owning himself too weak to dare
   A brother's hostile face,
Too weak to stand alone and fight
Against the strong world's might with right—
   A leader's part to take;
Dying a daily death in life,
At outward peace and inward strife,
   For poor convention's sake.

10

Let organ music swell and peal,
   And priests and people pray,
Let those who can at altar kneel—
   I have no heart to stay.
I cannot bear to see it done—
This fresh young life, scarce yet begun,
   Closed by that iron door;
A free-born spirit gagged and bound,
Tethered to one small plot of ground,
While all the great world spreads around,
   And doomed to fly no more.

'Australie'

(Emily Manning)

From the Clyde to Braidwood

A winter morn. The blue Clyde river winds
'Mid sombre slopes, reflecting in clear depths
The tree-clad banks or grassy meadow flats
Now white with hoary frost, each jewell'd blade
With myriad crystals glistening in the sun.

Thus smiles the Vale of Clyde, as through the air
So keen and fresh three travellers upward ride
Toward the Braidwood heights. Quickly they pass
The rustic dwellings on the hamlet's verge,
Winding sometimes beside the glassy depths
Of Nelligen Creek, where with the murmuring bass
Of running water sounds the sighing wail
Of dark swamp-oaks, that shiver on each bank;
Then winding through a shady-bower'd lane,
With the flickering streaks of sunlight beaming through
The feathery leaves and pendant tassels green
Of bright mimosa, whose wee furry balls
Promise to greet with golden glow of joy
The coming spring-tide.

          Now a barren length
Of tall straight eucalyptus, till again
A babbling voice is heard, and through green banks
Of emerald fern and mossy boulder rocks,
The Currawong dances o'er a pebbly bed,
In rippling clearness, or with cresting foam
Splashes and leaps in snowy cascade steps.
Then every feature changes—up and down,
O'er endless ranges like great waves of earth,
Each weary steed must climb, e'en like a ship
Now rising high upon some billowy ridge
But to plunge down to mount once more, again
And still again.

          Naught on the road to see
Save sullen trees, white arm'd, with naked trunks,

And hanging bark, like tatter'd clothes thrown off,
An undergrowth of glossy zamia palms
Bearing their winter store of coral fruit,
And here and there some early clematis,
Like starry jasmine, or a purple wreath
Of dark kennedea, blooming o'er their time,
As if in pity they would add one joy
Unto the barren landscape.

But at last
A clearer point is reach'd, and all around
The loftier ranges loom in contour blue,
With indigo shadows and light veiling mist
Rising from steaming valleys. Straight in front
Towers the Sugarloaf, pyramidal King
Of Braidwood peaks.

Impossible it seems
To scale that nature-rampart, but where man
Would go he must and will; so hewn from out
The mountain's side, in gradual ascent
Of league and half of engineering skill
There winds the Weber Pass.

A glorious ride!
Fresher and clearer grows the breezy air,
Lighter and freer beats the quickening pulse
As each fair height is gain'd. Stern, strong, above
Rises the wall of mountain; far beneath,
In sheer precipitancy, gullies deep
Gloom in dark shadow, on their shelter'd breast
Cherishing wealth of leafage richly dight
With tropic hues of green.

No sound is heard
Save the deep soughing of the wind amid
The swaying leaves and harp-like stems, so like
A mighty breathing of great mother earth,
That half they seem to see her bosom heave
With each pulsation as she living sleeps.
And now and then to cadence of these throbs
There drops the bell-bird's knell, the coach-whip's crack,
The wonga-pigeon's coo, or echoing notes
Of lyre-tail'd pheasants in their own rich tones,
Mocking the song of every forest bird.

Higher the travellers rise—at every turn
Gaining through avenued vista some new glimpse
Of undulating hills, the Pigeon-house
Standing against the sky like eyrie nest
Of some great dove or eagle. On each side
Of rock-hewn road, the fern trees cluster green,
Now and then lighted by a silver star
Of white immortelle flower, or overhung
By crimson peals of bright epacris bells.

Another bend, a shelter'd deepening rift,
And in the mountain's very heart they plunge—
So dark the shade, the sun is lost to view.
Great silver wattles tremble o'er the path,
Which overlooks a glen one varying mass
Of exquisite foliage, full-green sassafras,
The bright-leaf'd myrtle, dark-hued Kurrajong
And lavender, musk-plant, scenting all the air,
Entwined with clematis or bignonia vines,
And raspberry tendrils hung with scarlet fruit.

The riders pause some moments, gazing down,
Then upward look. Far as the peeping sky
The dell-like gully yawns into the heights;
A tiny cascade drips o'er mossy rocks,
And through an aisle of over-arching trees,
Whose stems are dight with lichen, creeping vines,
A line of sunlight pierces, lighting up
A wealth of fern trees; filling every nook
With glorious circles of voluptuous green,
Such as, unview'd, once clothed the silent earth
Long milliards past in Carboniferous Age.

A mighty nature-rockery! Each spot
Of fertile ground is rich with endless joys
Of leaf and fern; now here a velvet moss,
And there a broad asplenium's shining frond
With red-black veinings or a hart's-tongue point,
Contrasting with a pale-hued tender brake
Or creeping lion's-foot. See where the hand
Of ruthless man hath cleft the rock, each wound
Is hidden by thick verdure, leaving not
One unclothed spot, save on the yellow road.

Reluctant the travellers leave the luscious shade
To mount once more. But now another joy—
An open view is here! Before them spreads
A waving field of ranges, purple grey,
In haze of distance with black lines of shade
Marking the valleys, bound by a line
Of ocean-blue, o'er whose horizon verge
The morning mist-cloud hangs. The distant bay
Is clear defined. The headland's dark arms stretch
(Each finger-point white-lit with dashing foam)
In azure circlet, studded with rugged isles—
A picturesque trio, whose gold rock sides glow
In noonday sunlight, and round which the surf
Gleams like a silvery girdle.

                              The grand Pass
Is traversed now, the inland plateau reach'd,
The last sweet glimpse of violet peaks is lost,
An upland rocky stream is pass'd and naught
But same same gum-trees vex the wearied eye
Till Braidwood plain is reach'd.

                              A township like
All others, with its houses, church, and school—
Bare, bald, prosaic—no quaint wild tower,
Nor ancient hall to add poetic touch,
As in the dear old land—no legend old
Adds softening beauty to the Buddawong Peak,
Or near-home ranges with too barbarous names.
But everything is cold, new, new, too new
To foster poesy; and famish'd thought
Looks back with longing to the mountain dream.

The Two Beaches—Manly

Ocean

Thundering rolls the storming ocean, foaming on the golden sand,
Rising high in purple anger, frowning on the silent land;
Ridge on ridge of heaving billows, buoy'd upon a giant breast
Palpitating with a passion of eternal fierce unrest.
Manlike in its daring fervour, grand in savageness of force,
That must break or self be broken by whate'er shall mar its course:
Now its utmost force it gathers, deep a mighty sob resounds,
In one surging arc of waters, res'lute to o'erburst its bounds.

Vain! The war-plumed heads must lower, Nature's law shall be
    obey'd:
'Thus far, never farther!' conquers; prone the haughty waves are
    laid,
Humbled, frothing with the struggle, sweeping in, then backward
    drawn,
Leaving but the tiny furrow that their utmost throes have worn.

See, the western sun is sinking, grim the stolid headlands gloom.
Rising dark above the spray-smoke and the loud attacking boom
Of the cannonade of waters, lit with fire of sunset gold,
While the glory-mists of evening bays and hillsides sweet enfold.
Glare the rocks their salt-tear'd parting, earth in quiet slumber
    rests,
Yet th' impatient waves are fretting, still they lift their wrathful
    crests,
Moving black with ghostly aureoles, like a mighty spirit doom'd
Ne'er to cease its warring stuggle while the endless ages loom'd,
So it lasheth; seething, panting, with one deep despairing roar,
Image of the world's unquiet, knowing peace for nevermore.

Harbour

Calmly, gently, rock the waters, smiling in a maze of blue,
Womanlike, in love reflecting every changing light and hue;
Sometimes creeping into shadow, near a strong protective head,
Then in glistening joy of ripples into wooing sunshine led.
Or like a child at sport with lions, casting silvery shower of spray,
On hard-featured rocks that, moveless, stern resist their graceful
    play.

Pass the wavelets careless sweetly o'er the lake's still-breathing
    breast,
Troubled whiles at Ocean's portals by the billow's threatening
    crest,
Then once more their smile regaining, dancing on with gladsome
    speech,
Till they lay their emerald crescents fondly on the haven'd beach.
Storming not, nor scarcely whispering, but with kiss and lapping
    feet,
Rise the waters to their tide-height, with unnoted swiftness meet,
Rarely leaving mark or token where the crystal steps have been,
Yet fulfilling all their portion with a noiseless strength unseen;
Ebbing, flowing, as the Ocean in its due appointed hour,
But like force of love contrasted with the rage of restless power.

Sunlight's tints have paled to neutral, toned to hues of soothing
grey,
And in hallow'd trance of stillness Nature ends her chequer'd day;
Black th' embracing lands are profiled clear against the evening sky,
Throwing up by darksome setting lucent deeps which quivering lie
Like a liquid sea of opal, hoarding every dying beam,
And with answering light reflecting early stars that faintly gleam,
Till the goodnight darkness falleth, and with breath of rippling
sound,
Dreaming wavelets, slumb'rous murmuring, 'neath the spell of
sleep are bound.

Mary Hannay Foott

Where the Pelican Builds

The horses were ready, the rails were down,
    But the riders lingered still,—
        One had a parting word to say,
    And one had his pipe to fill.
Then they mounted, one with a granted prayer,
    And one with a grief unguessed.
        'We are going' they said, as they rode away—
    'Where the pelican builds her nest!'

They had told us of pastures wide and green,
    To be sought past the sunset's glow;
        Of rifts in the ranges by opal lit;
    And gold 'neath the river's flow.
And thirst and hunger were banished words
    When they spoke of that unknown West;
        No drought they dreaded, no flood they feared,
    Where the pelican builds her nest!

The creek at the ford was but fetlock deep
    When we watched them crossing there;
        The rains have replenished it thrice since then
    And thrice has the rock lain bare.
But the waters of Hope have flowed and fled,
    And never from blue hill's breast
        Come back—by the sun and the sands devoured—
    Where the pelican builds her nest!

In the Land of Dreams

A bridle-path in the tangled mallee,
  With blossoms unnamed and unknown bespread,—
And two who ride through its leafy alley,—
  But never the sound of a horse's tread.

And one by one whilst the foremost rider
  Puts back the boughs which have grown apace,—
And side by side where the track is wider,—
  Together they come to the olden place.

To the leaf-dyed pool whence the mallards fluttered,
  Or ever the horses had paused to drink;
Where the word was said and the vow was uttered
  That brighten for ever its weedy brink.

And Memory closes her sad recital,—
  In Fate's cold eyes there are kindly gleams—
While for one brief moment of blest requital,—
  The parted have met,—in the Land of Dreams.

Honora Frances Kelly

'King Jimmy'

(Colonial Idyll of the King)

Upon his bare breast's sable plain,
Suspended by its burnished chain,
Behold the brazen crescent swing
That marks its wearer as a king;
A king cross-legg'd upon the ground,
Whom grandeur doth not hedge around,
For state's grave cares but lightly press
Upon this son of the wilderness.
His crown was once a ruddy band,
Wrought by the slim and supple hand
Of mate he lov'd—it well may be—
Some fond, though black, Penelope;
A fillet woven stout and strong,
From fibre of the kurrajong;

But that was long ago—hats now
Of varied fashion grace his brow.
Now 'tis the martial helmet neat
Of the smartest man upon the 'beat',
Or next some swell's white 'billy-cock'
That oft in 'big-smoke' did the block.
Felts, hard-hitters, and—pray don't smile—
Sometimes a yachtsman's natty 'tile'!
Those eyes purblind, were falcon-bright,
To follow once the spear's swift flight;
Or from the grassy plain or hill
Saw 'boom'rang' hurl'd with subtle skill,
That slim, light crescent, that could fly
Like some swift bird thro' summer sky,
Whose sender, when it backward came
Dismay'd pursued his quest of game.
Ah! once swift tiny 'native' bee,
Poor Jimmy's eyes were first to see!
A sage old king, who well, I trow,
Can conjugate the verb 'to know'
Far better than celestial wight
Who deems that phrase his own, by right!
Marsupials all he doth eschew,
For 'myall' forebears, though they'd do;
He votes e'en 'possum ro-co-co,
The chosen patter long ago.
White-fellow's beeves have far more savour,
Merino 'tops' with him find favour;
Lean meat or tough likes not, I ween,
This king, who's his own 'chef cuisine'!
Of tea and sugar, bread, and 'duff'
From subjects, he might have enough,
E'en tho' our good Queen did not give
Him rations whereupon to live.
And from the same most gracious hand
(God spare her long, who rules this land)
An annual blanket welcome is,
And soothing to his 'rheumatiz';
For he is now infirm and old,
And keenly feels the winter's cold,
And else, would shiver in the wind,
His 'gunyah's' tiny far behind
On things the best long live, poor king!
Still snatches of weird war-chant's sing,
While phantom 'lubra's' fingers beat

In fancy, time to stamping feet
Of warriors, who in vanish'd days—
Illum'd by scatter'd 'wee-wee's' blaze—
Made splendid show in warlike dance,
With stiffen'd muscles, fierce, wild glance.
Alas! poor sable savage crew,
Fleet-lim'd and supple, where are you?
Ah! well may Jimmy's clouded brow
And wistful glance ask vainly now!
Still by his fire, at eve he sees—
Flamelit—the trunks of great gum trees,
Mid whose white boles, flit to and fro,
The vanish'd hosts of long ago.
The mystic 'Boro's' secret rite
Is still a dream of his delight,
Though youngsters of the camp scarce claim
Acquaintance with its hollow name;
Erstwhile the magic crucible
That youthful manhood tested well,
An ordeal stern, whose mystery
No 'lubra's' eye might ever see.
The years beyond three score and ten
Can blanch the locks of wise white men;
But unlike thee, poor grizzl'd king,
Our 'grand old men' but seldom sing;
Thou beat'st them there, poor harmless son
Of Austral's clime, whose race is run—
Or nearly so—who'll soon have found
His forebear's 'happy hunting ground'.

Louisa Lawson

Coming Home

Going round the back street,
   Through the twilight lane,
While the folk at church meet—
   Coming home again.

Faded hat and creasy,
   Long since it was new;
Tent-fly torn and greasy,
   Bluey showing through.

Billy burnt and battered,
  Boots all badly burst,
Lace and lace-holes shattered,
  Trousers at their worst.

Blankets like a riddle,
  With a streak of white
Down the threadbare middle
  When against the light.

Young face lined and sunburnt,
  Hair just turning grey;
Many a lesson unlearnt
  Since he went away.

But he need not bother,
  There's a bite and sup;
And for all the other—
  Mother'll fix him up.

A Pound a Mile

The tar-boy looked perplexed to see
  Tom Dawson cut the skin,
And Sweeper Bill remarked that he
  Had nothing in the bin.

His eyes for want of sleep were red,
  And slow his shears did click,
And whispers went around the shed
  That Dawson's wife was sick.

Then kindly spoke old Daddy Tonk:
  'Don't look so glum, my lad;
Is she, your missus, very cronk?'
  'Yes, mate,' said Tom, 'she's—bad.'

'Are there no women on the place?
  There should be two or three.'
'There are, but in my poor wife's case
  They say they're "all at sea."

'Then bring a doctor,' Daddy said;
   'Don't let the woman die!'
But Tommy Dawson hung his head
   And made him no reply.

'Get Pile to come out if you can,
   He'll pull the missus through.
Spend all you can to save her, man,
   I would if I were you.'

Then Dawson looked up from the ground,
   And white his features grew:
'Look, mate! If you had not a pound
   Now tell me what you'd do?'

'What would it cost then, now, to send
   And fetch out Dr Pile?
Some of the men the cash would lend.'
   Tom groaned, 'A pound a mile.'

'That's stiff, by God!' said Monty Styles,
   'The doctor does it brown;
There's sixty-five, I know, good miles
   Between us and the town.'

'It is a "coo-ey" with her now,'
   Said Dawson, in despair.
'I cannot save her anyhow—
   I'm euchred everywhere.'

Then up sprang Maori, on the job—
   'Here, look, see! There's my quid.
And here, look, see! So help me bob!
   There's two from Dick and Syd.'

And in his hat the money fell
   From willing hands and free.
'A quid a mile,' said Barney Bell;
   'Here goes! I'll give yer three.'

The Boss said, 'Put me down for ten,
   And catch the blood mare, Ted—
And put her in the sulky then—
   Don't wait till she is fed.

'Now, wire the doctor, quick, to come,
    And meet me mile for mile;
And, Tommy, man, hold up, old chum.'
    (Poor Tommy tried to smile.)

The squatter lit his pipe with care
    And drew his chin-strap in,
Then took his seat and touched the mare
    And started for the spin.

Then slow the hours of night went by
    To those around the shed,
For not a man had closed an eye,
    Not one had gone to bed.

'She's sinking now,' the women said,
    'She can't much longer last;
Before an hour she will be dead,
    Her strength is failing fast.'

'I'll go and let the sliprails down,'
    The black boy slowly said,
For far along the road to town
    He heard a horse's tread.

Then everyone sprang up and bent
    A watchful eye and ear,
And soon the boss a 'coo-ey' sent
    To show that he was near.

Then in the middle of the night
    The blood mare, limping, came
All tucked and blown, and wet and white,
    And panting hard, but game.

The doctor quick and silently
    Then with the women went,
And very soon a baby's cry
    Was heard in Dawson's tent.

'Thank God,' he said, 'My work is done,'
    As Tommy's hand he pressed;
'I've saved your wife and little son,
    Let nature do the rest.'

And then they went into the shed—
　　The men and Dr Pile—
And drank his health in Queensland red,
　　And paid him—pound for mile.

Catherine Martin

By the Blue Lake of Mount Gambier

Guarded by rugged banks and drooping trees
Beneath whose shade, far down, the waters sleep,
Clear as a mirror, countless fathoms deep,
Ne'er stirred by aught, saving the straying breeze
That warily passes, as by stealth, to meet
The rising ripples that with sapphire gleam,
Come softly, as one moving in a dream,
And on the grey old rocks untiring beat—
Glancing like priceless pearls in the still noon,
When smit by the great sun's too ardent rays;
Mirroring back at night the queenly moon,
When through grand legions of calm stars she strays,—
Peaceful, yet never still, they fall and rise
With a low strain, broken by slumb'rous sighs.
How oft and gladly have I sought the scene
To sit alone upon the sheltered bank,
While wearying cares into oblivion sank,
As the grand calmness of those depths serene
Fell with a healing power upon my heart,
Till the trite nothings that men hold so dear—
Cherish with gratitude, and guard with fear,
As if in them they held the better part—
Shrank into utter emptiness away!
Majestic Nature's peace there I have sought
And found, and there the unchecked flow of thought
Has led my soul afar. There day by day
I heard the twitter of the fearless birds,
Building their nests and singing griefless songs,
Within white blossomed bushes, in gay throngs,
Safe from discordant noises, jarring words.
And thus one day, as lying in the shade,
With head uplifted, resting on my hand,
I saw with dreamy rapture the fair land
That summer's presence fairer still had made.
The golden harvest fields from east to west

Stretch'd, fram'd by the still woods, while far and near
Lay peaceful homesteads. Anon sweet and clear
Came sound of bells from pastures, where to rest
And browse the tired oxen strayed. On hill
And dale December's golden presence shone
In the great gifts she had so largely strown.
Then when my grateful eyes had gazed their fill,
A weakly chirping fell upon my ear,
And half wonderingly I looked around,
To see a small brown bird upon the ground,
Hopping with fluttering wings and notes of fear;
Its ruffled feathers and its glazing eyes
Told that its end was drawing very near;
And still it pecked 'mid leaves that were long sere,
While ever and anon, with shrill, weak cries,
It looked upon a spreading prickly bush,
That with its honey-scented bloom grew nigh,
From which at last I heard a piping cry,
And idly thought—'The dying bird must wish,
With those shrill cries, to waken its dull mate,
That seems to doze within yon leafy screen.'
Then as I watched the bush I saw between
Two curving twigs a nest; within it wait
Three half-fledged birds, whose beaks were open'd wide,
While with big wondering eyes they look'd around;
Then as they heard the chirping weakly sound
Made by the parent bird, from side to side
They turned with hungry eyes, until at last
They saw her with weak drooping wings arise;
But now she falls, and yet again she tries
To fly unto her nest, and ever cast
Piteous looks towards her callow brood,
Holding the while a morsel in her beak;
With a last effort, and a low shrill squeak
She fluttered to the nest, and proudly stood
Upon its edge, giving to each a share;
But ere one happy moment thus had sped
She trembled, backward swayed, and then fell dead.
The young ones piped for food, but she lay there
With upward pointing, stiffening little claws,
And spreading ruffled wings, that never more
Would float upon the air. Then, very sore
At heart, I said—'For fear unholy paws
Of prowling cats may desecrate thy rest,
Here, noble mother, will I make a grave
(Where the clematis' blossoms gladly wave)

For thee, just underneath the little nest
That thou mad'st in the spring.' But there, above
The mother's tomb, the young ones piped for food,
Until I sadly thought—'It was not good
To lay the mother there, for her great love
Was such, that even in the cloudless clime
Where her freed spirit floats in sunny bliss,
Those cries will reach her, and destroy her peace.'
And then I formed a plan—I looked some time,
Till a few worms I found, with which I fed
The hungry orphans. Then from day to day
I gave them food till they had flown away
On vigorous wings. There ever as I sped
To my young noisy charges, beauties new
Disclosed themselves, around the calm grand lake
That softly bright, as heaven's own blue doth break
Beneath great banks and trees upon the view.
In the sweet hush of morn, when sun rays stole
Athwart it from the east with rosy glow,
While the trees and bushes jubilant grow
With hymns of countless birds, that upward roll
O'er hum of insects, fluttering of leaves:—
When in the ecstatic hour of fervid noon,
The sun-embraced earth lies, as in a swoon
Of overwhelming bliss: through silent eves
Of solemn gladness, when tones from afar
Of home-returning labourers, through the hush
Are heard, when the day's heat and eager rush
Once more are past, and the great evening star
Is brightening in the gold-swath'd west: in each
And every hour the long-known, well-loved scene
A holy sanctuary to me has been,
Where lessons, that no mortal tongue could teach,
Nor any book unfold, upon my soul
Have sunk. Full well I know no other spot
More dear to me may be: although my lot
May yet be cast afar, yet through the roll
Of coming years, forgetfulness' dull mist
Will never cloud the scene—never efface
The picture of the gleaming, amethyst,
Clear, rippling depths, o'er which with tender grace
The grandly swelling banks stoop proudly round,
As if to guard the Lake from each rude sound,
And keep inviolate the holy peace
That seems like a foretaste of Heaven's bliss.

Mary Gilmore

Aboriginal Themes

(i) THE CALL

We dwell not among the women as the white men do.
We are the hunters; we follow the call
Of the forest and the tracks therein;
Ours is the way of the bird and the kangaroo.
But the women dwell apart; they have a world
Into which we do not enter, save
When the life call speaks.
Then we answer it.

(ii) AT DAWN

At dawn I stood to see the sun come up;
He came like the face of a man
Proud from the hunting;
Like a man who says, 'There is food!'
And the food feeds his people.

(iii) IN THE NIGHT

In the night I saw the stars,
And the stars were like
The eyes of women
Seen through the leaves.
In the night I saw flash forth
The moonbeams from a possum's eyes;
Bright in the dark
They were the eyes of my woman.

(iv) FALLING FEATHERS

Once, when the world was young, we were a people;
Then came the white man to this our land.
Now we are like falling feathers,
The feathers of a wounded bird.

(v) CIVILIZED

I was a singer in a tree,
I was an eagle in the height,
From my shoulders shot the spear-heads of the sun—
Who now am but a caged bird with a broken wing.

(vi) A LAMENT

Beat the breast and cry,
Ai! . . . Ai! . . . Ai! . . .

Our friend is dead!
Our bitter bread
With us he shared;

Now he is dead
Who with us fared;
Beat the breast and cry,
Ai! . . . Ai! . . . Ai! . . .

(vii) WHEN THE BLACKS WEPT ME

A-ee! . . . A-ee! . . . A-ee! . . .
She was a child,
But we loved her,
And she loved us.
She was with us
And was happy;
Now she goes away,
And we shall see her no more.
Heavy are our hearts at her going.
In her departure we weep.
A-eee! . . . A-eee! . . . A-eee! . . .

(viii) NIGHT

The sun sinks slowly down;
Darkens the forest;
The shadows lengthen and run on the grass,
Or like great birds they fall.
In the trees naught moves but a leaf,
Twisting and turning;
Naught sounds but the click of a beetle,
Upward slow creeping.

Swift through the twilight
Like a grey phantom,
Silent the wallaroo
Glides in his going.

Now, like a bird on the nest,
Night feathers the earth;
In the far heavens
Sharpen the stars.

Never Admit the Pain

Never admit the pain,
   Bury it deep;
Only the weak complain,
   Complaint is cheap.

Cover thy wound, fold down
   Its curtained place;
Silence is still a crown,
   Courage a grace.

The Hunter of the Black

Softly footed as a myall, silently he walked,
All the methods of his calling learned from men he stalked;
Tall he was, and deeply chested, eagle-eyed and still,
Every muscle in his body subject to his will.

Dark and swarthy was his colour; somewhere Hampshire born;
Knew no pity for the hunted, weakness met his scorn;
Asked no friendship, shunned no meetings, took what life might
   bring;
Came and went among his fellows something like a king;

Paid each debt with strict exactness, what the debt might be;
Called no man employed him master; master's equal, he;
Yet there was not one who sought him, none who held his hand;
Never father calling, bid him join the family band.

Tales and tales were told about him, how, from dawn till dark,
Noiselessly he trailed his quarry, never missed a mark,
How the twigs beneath his footstep 'moved but never broke',
How the very fires he kindled 'never made a smoke'.

Men would tell with puzzled wonder, marked on voice and brow,
How he'd stand a moment talking, leave, and none knew how;
'*He was there!*' and then had vanished, going as he came,
Like the passing of a shadow, like a falling flame.

Once (I heard it when it happened,) word was sent to him,
Of a lone black on Mimosa—O the hunting grim!
Through three days and nights he tracked him, never asking sleep;
Shot, for him who stole the country, him who killed a sheep.

Tomahawk in belt, as only adults needed shot,
No man knew how many notches totalled up his lot;
But old stockmen striking tallies, rough and ready made,
Reckoned on at least a thousand, naming camps decayed.

Time passed on, and years forgotten whitened with the dust;
He whose hands were red with slaughter sat among the just,
Kissed the children of his children, honoured in his place,
Turned and laid him down in quiet, asking God his grace.

Nationality

I have grown past hate and bitterness,
I see the world as one;
But though I can no longer hate,
My son is still my son.

All men at God's round table sit,
And all men must be fed;
But this loaf in my hand,
This loaf is my son's bread.

Fourteen Men

Fourteen men,
And each hung down
Straight as a log
From his toes to his crown.

Fourteen men,
Chinamen they were,
Hanging on the trees
In their pig-tailed hair

Honest poor men,
But the diggers said 'Nay!'
So they strung them all up
On a fine summer's day.

There they were hanging
As we drove by,
Grown-ups on the front seat,
On the back seat I.

That was Lambing Flat,
And still I can see
The straight up and down
Of each on his tree.

The Lesser Grail

1

I have no thunder in my words,
    Thunder is much too high;
But I can see as far as birds,
    And feel the wind go by.

And I can follow through the grass
    The darling-breasted quail;
For, though things great in splendour mass
    I choose the lesser grail.

Age changes no one's heart; the field
    Is wider, that is all.
Childhood is never lost; concealed,
    It answers every call.

So when the wind goes bloring by,
    And in the driving hail,
Or when the tempest shakes the sky,
    I run beside the quail.

2

The willow by the fountain
    Is just a willow-tree,
But I have seen it billow
    As though it were the sea.

And sometimes, in the spring,
    It seemed a woman's hair,
Tossed, and wanton-minded,
    As it played on the air.

Wintered I have seen it,
    And oh, it was human,
Crying on the wind
    Like an old grey woman.

3

The butterfly went lightly over,
Flower by flower, as though a lover;
And yet it had no thought of love
For any flower it poised above.

The quail upon her little feet,
Ran in and out amid the wheat,
Entreating me lest I should tread
Where love had made its breast a bed.

Mary E. Fullerton

Crows

At an old water-hole,
Bones lay in the hide
And teeth gibbered up
Of things that had died.

Tortured of thirst,
There came to the mud
A son of the plain,
Who sank where he stood.

Then the crows from afar,
Where the water was good,
Came nearer, for heaven
Had given them food.

Vandal

The farmer on the river, by the bend,
Has killed the wattles that I loved last Spring!
The thrush, too, loved them, and the quick fantail;
The warbling magpie, and the shy bronzewing.

Their healing effluence on my heart they spilt,
Upon my soul, long arid in her drouth;
Softly the blossoms touched, like virgin kiss,
My weary eyelids and my parched mouth.

And now I see the dying stems exude
The trees' last sap, and I, the heart they healed,
Behold their doom and can do nought to save
The riven magic of September's yield.

The birds are gone, and on the landscape's face
The sun smites down, unmitigably stark,
And in his waggon on the road near by
The farmer bears his load of vandalled bark.

Contented with his pipe, he bumps along,
Unwitting that among those withered sheaves
He bears bird twitters, and the golden dreams
My dry heart gathered under golden eaves.

War Time

Young John, the postman, day by day,
In sunshine or in rain,
Comes down our road with words of doom
In envelopes of pain.

What cares he as he swings along
At his mechanic part,
How many times his hand lets fall
The knocker on a heart?

He whistles merry scraps of song,
What'er his bag contain—
Of words of death, of words of doom
In envelopes of pain.

Comet

The comet that my father saw,
His breathing sons will never see,
So vast his journey, and so brief
Their poor inept mortality.

Why went that speeding majesty
Along the unplumbed planes of air,
And over what unpictured hills
Still flash his maddened manes of hair?

What embassage compels his speed?
They only know, those drudging seers,
That he will burn beyond our eyes
For fifty of our human years.

And all that time he rides, he rides:
The hidden rowels urge like doom,
Then, from undated ways of space
He hurtling on our skies shall come.

And men shall watch, and he shall go,
No cosmic message caught, or given,
Dumb as the jealous seraphim,
Who hide beyond the cloak of heaven.

Body

We fend for this poor thing,
Wash, dress, and give it food,
Love it before all men
Through each vicissitude.

Give it whate'er it ask,
Shield it from heat and cold,
And croon above its pains
When time has made it old.

It is but house and home
That for no term we rent;
We seldom talk with Him—
Its mighty resident.

Body's the easy one,
That lets the mortal be,
As though the pretty shell
Were the essential He.

Sometimes in hardihood,
We touch the inner door—
Two entities in one.
Visited and visitor.

Oh, Tenant of my flesh,
I knock, and turn, and fly,
Afraid of the appraisement
Within that solemn eye.

Passivity

Call not on comfort lest she come
With all her helpers sleek and dumb—
Soft ropes that seem as frail as air,
To bind you in a cushioned chair,
With anodyne, and balm, and spell,
To chant of droning ritual.

Traffic with danger, heat, and strain,
Face when it comes the spear of pain:
None that achieve—the bad, the good—
Have sold to comfort, hardihood.

Oh, flaccid, havened, housed, defended,
Flesh still alive, but *living*, ended!
Angels nor devils are of these—
The castaways on velvet ease.

Mary Richmond

Sydney Harbour

(New Year's Eve, 1897)

The jewelled city glitters through the night,
  The jewelled boats glide softly through the gloom;
  On the either hand dark isles and headlands loom,
And overhead stars flood the heavens with light.

Our vessel trembles, as the bronze blades smite
  The quiet waters, and the engines urge
  Our forward way to where the sounding surge
Washes the cliff, and all the waves are white.

'Tis midnight; from the distant city spires;
  The bells peal out a welcome to the year,
And ruddy glows the smoke of festal fires.

The lighthouse now, unbonneted and free,
  Throws out pale spokes of light that wheel and veer,
And one great planet burns above the sea.

Marie E. J. Pitt

Reveille

Up! comrades, up! the night has flown,
  The dawn breaks dim and grey!
The bugle-call of strife has blown!
  Arm! arm you for the fray!
O'er hills which man's injustice smote,
  The People's hymn we'll raise,
Shout! every throat, a major note,
  Australia's Marseillaise!

They call our creed a rebel creed,
  Our flag a rebel flag,
Who scrawl the autograph of greed
  On every wave-worn crag;
Who sow in furrows of their greed
  A heritage of scorn,
And bind the bonds of bitter need
  On peoples yet unborn;

Who ruthless weave the fateful coil
  That binds in bonds of hate
Lean helotry of hopeless toil,
  Fat harlotry of State,
Who sow in furrows of their hate
  Twin thorns that never fail,
The gilded thieves in Church and State,
  The squalid thieves in gaol.

They call our flag a rebel flag,
  Our creed a rebel creed,
Who scrawl on every wave-worn crag
  The autograph of greed.
O'er hills which man's injustice smote,
  The People's hymn we'll raise,
Shout! every throat, a major note,
  Australia's Marseillaise!

The Reiver

The floods are out on the flats to-night
  Moaning and maddened and wild and red,
Like a ruthless slayer ready to smite,
  Old Mitchell rears in his straitened bed;
Quick! Lords of the cattle and crops, your dole!
The reiver river takes toll, takes toll!

Hope for no harvest of eager hands,
  The ripened ears and the swollen cribs!
The sludge-bar, tossed on the hungry sands,
  That gapes like a skeleton's sundered ribs,
The break and the blight and the far-flung shoal
Of the reiver river take toll, take toll!

The lean teams lagged at the furrow end,
  And the plumed green army stood brave anon,
Now from mourning upland to river bend
  The whisper is hushed and the plumes are gone,
Only the waters a death-dirge roll
Where the reiver river takes toll, takes toll!

Plunder, full plunder of horn and hoof,
  Of torn green tresses and whitening bone,
And a darker tribute, deep housed aloof
  Where the vespering pines on the hillside moan,
Man, beast and bird, and the twisted bole —
So the reiver river takes toll, takes toll!

The floods are out on the flats to-night,
  Pray if you dare to and hold your breath;
For a craft rides seaward with never a light,
  And the man at her wheel is Pilot Death.
Was it curlew or plover? Or parting soul?
Hush! — the reiver river takes toll, takes toll!

Australia's Tommy Atkins

(Written for the *Socialist*,
no apology to William Hamilton.)

O! we catch him young and make him a cadet,
   Give him side arms, and a rifle in his hand,
Tell him bogey yarns of heroes we have met,
   And the duty that he owes his native land;
He drinks it in with other things at school,
   That to keep the Old Flag flying cock-a-hoop,
He must learn the art of slaughter,
Learn to spill red blood like water,
   Tho' he lives in Melbourne Town or Dandaloop.

Refrain
   O! Tommy, Tommy Atkins,
     Will you never gather sense?
Will you never see the folly
     And the scandalous expense
Of the waste of time and labour
     That fits you for the trade
For the blood and thunder calling
     Of the Boodle Bug Brigade?

Yes! we take him from his football and his horse,
   From Tote, and Tate and snares of Mr Wren,
And we make of him a unit in the force
   That has learnt the noble game of killing men.
O! he's happy as a lunatic at play,
   With his buttons and his regulation suit,
When he's learnt to do his duty
For Profit, Power and Booty—
   When he's learnt the god of human life is loot.

O! we tell him of the grand Union Jack,
   Of the flag that speaks of Justice overseas,
How it swoops upon the lazy loafing black,
   Fat and happy 'neath his laden plantain trees,
How it chains him to the mattock and the hoe,
   For his sloth and shiftless folly to atone,
Till in bright anticipation,
We have grown so great a nation,
   That we've lots of pauper labour of our own.

And when he's done and can't fight any more
　We have him up before the local Beak,
And if he's got credentials to the fore,
　We pay him half a sovereign a week.
O! he'll live on it as happy as a king,
　For he knows he's done his duty like a man—
He is old and poor, and dying
But he kept the flag a-flying
　For Rob and Snob and all their caravan.

Autumn in Tasmania

White everlastings star the peaks again
Where mountain moss her living carpet spreads
And through the eaves of hollow runnel-beds
The soft sad winds of mourning March complain.
But yesterday through aisles of tasselled grain
Came Ceres singing—now grey gully-heads
Give back her grief. Like one in sleep she treads
And calls for lost Persephone in vain.

No glad voice answers. Olive-shadowed musk
Sheds funeral incense over ridge and fell
Where ebbed reluctant day; now like a ghost
A haggard moon rides up the eastern coast,
And through the silence, like a passing bell,
A bittern booms across the caverned dusk.

The Clan Call

I patted the head of a pony,
　By a Collins-street kerbstone tied,
And my soul is sick for the old things
　And the feel of the world outside.

I patted the head of a pony,
　My fingers are tingling yet;
And I hear the call of the outlands
　Ring over the city's fret.

He was low and little and weedy,
　But he bent his nose to my hand
In the language that never was written,
　That the horse-lovers understand.

And I feel the beck of the mountains,
   And the worn ways wandering white
Thro' the ironbarks and the messmates
   Are calling to me to-night.

And I ache in this city prison,
   In this desert of rolling roofs,
For the lift of snaffle and stirrup,
   For the ring of galloping hoofs,

'Mong the hills where the circling eagle
   Sails dark on the rim o' the day,
And the yang yangs' shrieking phalanx
   Heralds the stormy fray.

Flemington, Caulfield, Ascot?
   The Derby, the Melbourne Cup?
The seethe of the surging thousands?
   The steeds with their riders up?

They're tainted with craft of Commerce,
   By minions of Pelf they're ruled,
With a fig for the game outsider,
   And a curse for the nag that's 'pulled'.

'Twas a merrier sport and cleaner
   Where the ironstone ranges rung
To the race that never was written,
   To the steeds that never were sung.

'Twas a merrier sport and sweeter,
   The chestnut against the brown,
With the weight on the Gippsland gelding
   And a win for the mare, hands down.

On the open road we have won them,
   Close finish and hard-set teeth,
With God's own breath on our faces
   And His levin of life beneath.

On the open road we have lost them,
   Light-hearted and ridden away;
For there's never a game worth playing,
   Where the stake is more than the play.

Yes! I'm sick to-night for the old things
   That grip me like living hands,
In the dark of a world of shadows—
   And I know, while the old faith stands,

With the mate of my soul beside me,
   Light-hearted, without remorse,
I would tackle The Styx to-morrow
   On a fretting Australian horse.

'Sydney Partrige'

(Kate Margaret Stone)

Sund'y

Sund'y out here on th' s'lection,
   With nawthin' at all to do,
'Cept feed th' pigs an' th' chickens,
   An' pen up a poddy or two.

All right out here on th' s'lection,
   With nawthin' at all to do.
Th' sky seems 'sif you'd jest passed it
   Thro' a tub've mum's washin' blue.

Th' little clouds is like soap-suds
   'Tween us an' th' shiny sky.
There's a line've long-beaked ivers
   Flyin' lazy beyond our eye.

An' down to th' Cultivation
   Dad, Mum an' th' baby've gone,
To lean on th' sliprails admirin'
   Th' growth 've th' tasselin' cawn.

Blossom 'n' Gipsy 're standin'
   In th' shade 've th' ol' apple-gum
An' th' noise've th' leeks in th' branches
   Is mixed with th' honey-bees' hum.

An' me an' th' dawgs 'n' our Billy
  'N' a friendly neighbor or two,
Have a dead-ripe time on a Sund'y
  With nawthin' at all to do.

Capitalism

Ah, the song of the terrible bush,
Twelve sheep bogged where the grass grows lush,
Five crows caw on a ring-barked tree,
Droning their grace out thankfully;
Two glazing eyes in each dying head,
Five hungry crows that must be fed.
The Lord He gives and the Lord takes away—
My loss your gain when the last word's to say.
Capitalist Crow from his place on high
Swoops down to pick out each worker's eye,
Gorging his fill on the life-blood red,
Pitiless, heartless, unshamed by the dead.

Mabel Forrest

The Circus Lion

The spoil of cunning human hands,
  The tawny lion lies,
Dreaming, perchance, of desert sands,
  And far-off Lybian skies.

He sees the tombs of kings rise dark,
  The moonlight on the plain,
While a pale, narrow-shouldered clerk,
  Makes comments on his mane.

He rises, snarling at the hands,
  That point their feeble fun,
And longs upon the midnight sands,
  To see the red blood run.

He beats the rough boards with his tail,
　　His great jaws gnash their rage,
But what can royal strength avail,
　　Against a bar-set cage?

His muscles strain, his eyes grow dark,
　　He crouches for a spring. . . . .
Secure, the flaccid, weakling clerk,
　　Laughs at the Captive King!

Chaperones

With chilly feet and aching eyes, sitting against the wall,
Watching the budding beauties pass in triumph thro' the ball,
Watching the swirl of silken skirts, hearing the music moan,
Thinking of days when never feet were lighter than our own;
Thinking of eyes that looked in ours, eager for smile or word;
Thinking of tones of easy praise—half of a life unheard!
All the little a woman loves—all that she finds so much—
All the gossamer joys of youth—fled at the lean years' touch.
Grey-haired women, with wrinkled cheeks, have we forgotten all,
Do you think that we never dream—sitting against the wall?

Spectacled and over stout, heavy-cheeked, or thin and worn,
We are the twilight colourless; they are the rose-red morn;
Twilight muffles the reckless leap of quiv'ring young-old hearts,
As with drawn lips and mein severe, we play our thankless parts!
We have our scars—they throb and burn just as they used to do,
At the stir of a silken skirt—brush of a satin shoe.
Oh! sobbing music—that laughs for them, oh! wind in the oaks
　　outside,
We have been winsome maid and wife, and we have been shrinking
　　bride:
Death's is the one dance undanced, for us, who have footed all,
The last quadrille for veterans, sitting against the wall!

Peering thro' the painted net, and ivory of a fan,
The dim old eyes are clear once more, and the lips desired of man,
In the hush of velvet nights, 'neath the coronal of stars,
We hear the breeze go whimpering out by the black belars—
We are so old—so long unloved—shall we grow never wise,

As we droop our heads, remembering the magic of those skies?—
And then back to the lighted room, the sweet, last waltz begins,
The 'cello, with a waking sob, throbs thro' the violins.
To us it sings—as young love sang—a tender, deathless croon,
To the swing of swishing skirts, and the tap of pointed shoon!

Oh, dimpled maids, who play to-night, your merry mad-cap parts,
You, too, some day, with reckless leap of quiv'ring young-old
    hearts,
With wearied and remembering eyes, will sit against the wall,
And watch the budding beauties pass in triumph thro' the ball!

The Other Side

'I am busy sorting the morning's post,'
    Jonathan puts down his cup to say,
    'They're hanging a man at the jail to-day,'
And he helps himself to the buttered toast.

Thro' the lattice window there comes the call,
    Of sparrows chirping along the rail,
    A great Magnolia blossom pale,
Spreads its drowsy sweetness over all.

The grasses are long on the patch of lawn,
    Wild bees cling close to the hearts of flowers,
    A promise of warmer noon tide hours,
On the scented breeze from the north is borne.

And the children laugh with no sound of strife,
    As they pass to school on their loitering way,
    And every pulse of the summer's day,
Is a throb with the lusty force of life.

A dimpled daring, mischievous elf,
    One arm encircling his book and slate,
    Makes a snatch at a rosebud through the gate
And the clock strikes eight on the mantel shelf.

With no mourning train, and no church bell's toll,
    Where the prison walls rise rough and brown,
    The other side of the sunlit town,
They are setting a-drift a human soul.

Now Jonathan pushes the window wide,
  I pin in his coat a late blown rose,
  And out of the shady room he goes,
To the amber glare of the world outside.

I cannot help thinking, the while I note,
  The flowers that bloom and the birds that sing,
  Of that horrible, quiv'ring human thing,
And the cowering soul on the winds afloat.

The tendrilled wealth of a vine astray,
  To the clasp of the lattice frame is caught,
  I wish I could banish that haunting thought,
'They're hanging a man at the jail to-day!'

Kassaptu

(The Assyrian Witch)

The witch sits always in the shadow of the wall
  And under her blue robe she hides her hands
That never man may see the things she does at all,
  But my faint heart conceives and understands . . .
She is weaving Seven spells . . .
  Making flowers out of clay and scenting them too sweet,
For her voice is as the sound of Nippur bells
  Blowing to the desert from the street.

The witch sits in the shadow of the wall . . .
  And (braided like a warrior's of the race)
The midnight of her tresses seems to fall
  To blot the silver moonlight of her face . . .
Not a jewel does she carry on her amber throat and small,
  Every tooth she has is even, sharp and white—
I can see them when she's laughing in the shadow of the wall
  For she never once comes out into the light.

I have a Scythian lover, strong and tall,
  And the witch has many lovers. I have one—
I am languishing with fear lest he should pass this wall
  Coming in his chariot . . . out of Babylon.

Jean Logan Ranken

The First Night in Sydney Harbour

January 26th, 1788

Darkness has fallen over sea and land,
   The only lights are where the small fleet lies;
Dark forms are flitting on the wooded shores,
   From out the trees are peering frightened eyes.

Snatches of song are coming from the ships,
   Then peace, save for the tramp of sentries' feet,
Who through the night hours pace the storm worn decks,
   Eyes on th' new land, hearts in a London street.

A hundred years from now, a myriad lamps
   That glow like clustered gems, shall pierce the night,
Where now the densely wooded slopes are dark,
   A thousand homes shall rise and give their light.

For even now the black man takes his flight,
   He knows not why the strangers seek his shore,
But fear has waked, and stirs within his heart,
A dim forboding that his reign is o'er.

The water mirrors back the star-shot sky,
   Nor hints of future days, when to and fro
The ferry boats shall flit, their gleaming lights
   Dancing on waves where only stars now glow.

The soft waves lap the little sanded bays,
   The tall gums crown the heights, and seem to stand
Expectant of their doom, the white man comes,
   Their day is over, death is in his hand.

Where Nature for so long has held her sway,
   Home upon home will stand, and give their light.
Our children's children, living, loving then,
   Will they ere think of this first wond'rous night?

Where we see stretched before us, mile on mile,
   A masterpiece from out the master's hand,
A city soon will rise, and they who build,
   Seeing this beauty, needs must understand —

No chessboard city, planned by rule of thumb,
  But growing bit by bit as Nature grows,
With guarded spots where history laid a hand,
  And all the charm slow growing beauty knows—

Old ties are torn, we've come with hearts aglow,
  With hopes for all the unborn years to be,
When there shall rise the nation of our dreams,
  Strong in the power and might we shall not see.

We shall not see, but we shall plant the seeds
  Of that great future, and the heritage
Of those who follow us shall surely be
  Strength and endurance proved in this first age.

Sumner Locke

The Left Behinds

We're the Left Behinds, the Staybacks,
  We're the ones to catch the slack,
We're the class that's called Not Wanted,
  We're the virgins from Outback.
We're the hefty arm that's needed,
  We're the sort to feel the brunt,
We're the bloomin': 'Take your places
  While the men are at the front.'
So we're learnin' none too easy, under hand of heavy drought,
How to work and keep things lively when the men are ordered out.

An' they call us chicken-hearted,
  Sweatin' in the blessed sun,
Stickin' things and showin' merry,
  Tired as bullocks when it's done.
Drivin' plough and hoe and harrow,
  Facin' hell of every kind,
Tender spoke they used to know us,
  Now we've left it all behind.
So we're waking up to battle, battle, Lord, we're sure to get
Lonesome nights, and hungry children, rainless acres, hopeless debt.

'Rank Outsider,' 'Nom-de-Wayback,'
    Don't know nothin' of a gun.
What's the meanin' of a maxim?
    Shrapnel, lyddite (tell me, son)?
What's the trenches? Uhlans? Turcos?
    What's the bloomin' V.C. for?
What's recruits? And transport waggons?
    What's the game about—oh, Lor'!
So we're fightin' up the Mitchell, fightin' till we're most insane
Ants an' 'hoppers, weeds an' store-bills, hunger-ache and lack of
    rain.

Boots and bills, and things for children,
    Flies and 'skeetos, snakes and birds,
Starlings in the fruit at Xmas,
    Things for which there ain't no words;
Little debts the boss has shifted,
    Though he hasn't kicked them out,
Mortgage on the cows and horses,
    Nasty things to have about.
So it's us to do the fighting; in a sixteen-acre lot
Regiment's the bloomin' fam'ly, argument's the only shot.

Fightin', aren't we? Chivvyin' firewood,
    Kids at school and muddy tanks,
Cultivation gone to blazes,
    Want our men back? Well, no thanks,
We've stood in just where we started,
    Given more'n we ever got,
Couldn't work a hair's-breadth harder
    If the boss was home or not.
Such a fuss as they're a-makin'! If you's known us, you'd a-swore
Boss had heard his country callin', lots of other times before.

Chaps I know 'ave got commissions
    For His Majesty, the King,
P'r'aps it's guy or chaff, I'm thinkin',
    When they ain't done anything.
Seen up here at harvest picnics
    Playin' rounders with the girls,
Lord! to me it do seem funny
    Makin' chaps pretend they're earls.
'Services abroad,' that done it. Crikey! I've done service, too,
Rearing children, scrubbin' moleskins—things a man 'ud never do.

Bless yer, I can't see no difference
    Fightin' with a spade or gun.
Diggin' brings the kids their breakfast,
    That's a fight for anyone.
Killin' men in heathen countries,
    Stakin' out another lot,
Might be worth a fellow pluggin'
    If it kept a boilin' pot.
So it strikes me sudden, rather (sorry if you think I rouse),
But the fightin' started really right at home here, in our house.

Yet we're 'Left Behinds' and 'Staybacks,'
    Ready here to catch the slack,
Just the class that's called 'Not Wanted,'
    Blessed virgins from the back.
We're the anvil always heated,
    We're the bloomin' family tree,
We're the line for dirty washin',
    We're—just where we ought to be.
So I guess, without presumin', an' with just a little fuss,
To be fair to human bullocks, someone ought to mention us.

Ethel Anderson

From *Squatter's Luck*

Flood

From thick clouds over the black Warrumbungles,
And wracked, far-travelling Tambourine Mountains,
Red-earthed Jugiongs, steep Picton Razorbacks,
Rock-pierced, ice-weathered, snow-tossed Kosciusko,
    Autumnal sharp rains inundate the paddocks;

Infect with mildew the silk-tasselled maize-cobs,
Hurt more than seven years' drought the pastures,
Defile with seepage the claypanned waterholes;
Soon sluice down contours in the unsown fallows;
    Soon silt up creeks with alluvial wastage.

The water-hyacinth, treacherous, beautiful,
Mauve and merciless foe of fishermen,
The Creeping-Judas of soaks and billabongs,
Chokes up the channels, its tough seeds and stolons
    Increased by prolific multiplication.

Eroded then the buff shelved banks of Logan,
Lachlan, blue Hunter or swift-flowing Murray,
Denuded of oaks and grey eucalyptus,
Feathery sour-sapped bent-boughed melaleucas,
    Cave in; let spread the loud-snarling flood waters.

The young Australian at break of day gazing
Across a white gaggle of turbulent raindrops,
Sees his wheatrick dispersed, his corn-silo ruined,
Draggled, the plumes of his Brown Leghorn cockerel,
    From a floating hencoop crowing defiance.

He, seated at ease on the ridge of his roof,
Sees, drowned, his sheep; sees, perished, his prize cattle,
Sees on a frail raft his pale wife and children
Skirting the stack of his half-submerged homestead;
    Sees, twice sighs, and whistles 'Waltzing Matilda.'

Then tilts his ten-gallon cadie to windward,
And says to Eustace, his *fidus Achates*,
Humped in a sack on the coping beside him;
'OK for fodder, these red, bonzer rains are.'
    And Eustace intones to a queazy accordion.

Fire

From black clouds over the lost Warrumbungles,
Thick-hazed, invisible Tambourine Mountains,
Scarred Picton Razorbacks, burnt-out Jugiongs,
Dour and waterless slopes below Kosciusko
    Bush fires, blazing, obliterate the landscape.

Fan to cinders the tinder-dry turpentines,
Whip whistling down the wind faggots of stripped bark,
Fire whole townships to incandescent embers,
Leave lying dead in them seventy strong men,
    Dust on the ingots of the melted church bells.

In dreadful burned heaps piled in the waterholes,
Hundreds of kangaroos, wallabies, bandicoots;
Trapped in the tree-tops, phalangers, koalas;
Seared on the red-hot rocks, lizards, goannas,
    Yabbies, watersnakes; all die in this holocaust.

The frantic black swan covering her cygnets,
The Wonga pigeon, cowering on her nestlings,
The red foal, the fawn calf, myriads of butterflies
—Moonbeams, jewels, jezabels, and wood whites—
    All the bright, wild tribes of the bushland perish.

The young Australian, at set of sun looking
Across interminable, lurid furnaces,
Consumed, sees his silage; flaming, his wheatrick;
Gutted, his homestead; his live cattle roasted;
    Sees, and is silent. Fire is man's master.

So soused neck-high in a billabong shallow,
(His tired wife and children trembling beside him,
Eustace immersed in a neighbouring bolt-hole)
He sees the tongues of a raging tornado
    Sweep hungrily up to six hundred merinoes;

Huddled, the sheep are; the flames leap over them,
Blaze through the box boughs, glaze, scarlet, the distance.
A singed cock crows a jubilant 'a-doodle';
Left in a luke-warm rockcleft Eustace finds
    Twelve chocolate-brown eggs, a sitting Barnes-
      felder.

War

Through blue mists over the brown Warrumbungles,
Serene and shadowy Tambourine Mountains,
Green-skirted Jugiongs, moon-lit Razorbacks,
Dew-drenched, sun-kissed, fern-clad Kosciusko,
    The men from the land flock down in their thousands.

By push-bike, car, cart or utility-truck,
By pack-horse or train, plane, camel or sulky,
By bullock-dray, hay-waggon, Rolls-Royce, steamer,
Joy-riding, plodding on shanks' grey pony,
    The men from the land flock down in their thousands.

Active, deep-chested, virile, intelligent,
With massy thews worked to whip-cord by labour,
The best men God and their parents could perpetrate,
Eager to prove the true worth of their manhood,
    The men from the land flock down in their thousands.

'It's good-bye to the land!,' when war came, calmly,
Si said to Eustace: 'Our disc-plough's a Bren gun,
Our harrow's a tank,' 'Fighting Huns will be child's play
After our battles with fire, drought and flood, Si!'
    Enlisting, gaily, they too joined the army.

Sleeping Soldier

Dear love, I've seen you fast asleep,
   Twitched the green blind that screens the sun,
And sheathed the sword, once bright to reap
   The little sheaf your virtue won;

Your narrow bed's not made so strait
   That there's no room for me when, too,
I plumb the darkness where you wait,
   I go to lie nightlong by you.

'Anna Wickham'

(Edith Hepburn)

Divorce

A voice from the dark is calling me.
In the close house I nurse a fire.
Out in the dark cold winds rush free
To the rock heights of my desire.
I smother in the house in the valley below,
Let me out to the night, let me go, let me go.

Spirits that ride the sweeping blast,
Frozen in rigid tenderness,
Wait! for I leave the fire at last
My little-love's warm loneliness.
I smother in the house in the valley below,
Let me out to the night, let me go, let me go.

High on the hills are beating drums.
Clear from a line of marching men
To the rock's edge the hero comes
He calls me and he calls again.

On the hill there is fighting, victory or quick
　　death,
In the house is the fire, which I fan with sick
　　breath.
I smother in the house in the valley below,
Let me out to the dark, let me go, let me go.

The Marriage

What a great battle you and I have fought!
A fight of sticks and whips and swords,
A one-armed combat,
For each held the left hand pressed close to the
　　heart,
To save the caskets from assault.

How tenderly we guarded them;
I would keep mine and still have yours,
And you held fast to yours and coveted mine.
Could we have dropt the caskets
We would have thrown down weapons
And been at each other like apes,
Scratching, biting, hugging
In exasperation.

What a fight!
Thank God that I was strong as you,
And you, though not my master, were my match.
How we panted; we grew dizzy with rage.
We forgot everything but the fight and the love of
　　the caskets.

Those we called by great names —
Personality, Liberty, Individuality.

Each fought for right to keep himself a slave
And to redeem his fellow.
How can this be done?

But the fight ended.
For both was victory
For both there was defeat.
Through blood we saw the caskets on the floor.
Our jewels were revealed;
An ugly toad in mine,

While yours was filled with most contemptible
   small snakes:
One held my vanity, the other held your sloth.

The fight is over, and our eyes are clear.—
Good friend, shake hands.

Nettie Palmer

The Mountain Gully

Bracken breast-high beside the winding track,
   Sometimes a fallen log to bar the way,
A steep descent, the footing wet and black,
   The gully dewy-dark in burning day.

And there the hill-fed creek makes hidden play,
   A naiad half-discerned with smouldering eyes,
She holds a harp whose few slow notes betray
   The passion whence the ferns and mosses rise.

What ferns about the harp! What water plies
   In drops to make the music, on and on!
What deep content across the spirit lies
   Till all the world like floating dust is gone!

And you and I are here, and breathed upon
   By one enchantment . . . Ah, the hours betray!
And all the moving fingers of the sun
   Invade no more and tide-like shadows play.

We seek again the place of outer day,
   The long ascent, the footing wet and black,
Uncanny fallen logs to bar the way,
   Bracken aglow with sunset by the track.

The Barrack Yard

A sack of straw suspended from a tree,
   Soldiers with bayonets in the barrack yard,
   In turn they lunge and thrust and stand on guard,
Their faces rigid, fraught with destiny.

A summer wind is moving dreamily,
   The sack a hundred times is gashed and marred,
   In the tree-shadows by the railings barred
The city children stare and laugh to see.

What of life's glory, what of memory's glow!
What of the boon of song, the great word written,
   The highest peak our dreamers ever saw!
We learn to slay our kind. Ah, might we know,
Dying, that every foe our hands had smitten
   Was but a mute and soulless man of straw.

Dorothea Mackellar

My Country

The love of field and coppice,
   Of green and shaded lanes,
Of ordered woods and gardens
   Is running in your veins.
Strong love of grey-blue distance
   Brown streams and soft, dim skies—
I know but cannot share it,
   My love is otherwise.

I love a sunburnt country,
   A land of sweeping plains,
Of ragged mountain ranges,
   Of droughts and flooding rains.
I love her far horizons,
   I love her jewel-sea,
Her beauty and her terror—
   The wide brown land for me!

The stark white ring-barked forests,
   All tragic to the moon,
The sapphire-misted mountains,
   The hot gold hush of noon.
Green tangle of the brushes,
   Where lithe lianas coil,
And orchids deck the tree tops
   And ferns the warm dark soil.

Core of my heart, my country!
    Her pitiless blue sky,
When sick at heart, around us,
    We see the cattle die—
But then the grey clouds gather,
    And we can bless again
The drumming of an army,
    The steady, soaking rain.

Core of my heart, my country!
    Land of the Rainbow Gold,
For flood and fire and famine,
    She pays us back three-fold.
Over the thirsty paddocks,
    Watch, after many days,
The filmy veil of greenness
    That thickens as we gaze . . .

An opal-hearted country,
    A wilful, lavish land—
All you who have not loved her,
    You will not understand—
Though earth holds many splendours,
    Wherever I may die,
I know to what brown country
    My homing thoughts will fly.

Zora Cross

Love Sonnets

XVII

Belovèd, lest I should remember, I
Must swift forget the wonder of last night.
Hot memory would but blacken out my sight
And dull my senses till they seemed to die.
How could I live, remembering that sigh . . .
That breath . . . that sob . . . that all sublime
        delight?
Eternal joy is death, I think, and might
Not such sweet madness kill me, coming nigh?

I died with you that hour. Or, if not, merged
Myself in you, commingling all my life
Within your own, until I fled and fled
Into your blood; and my pure pulses surged,
Heaped with the wedded bliss of man and wife . . .
Dying, I lived . . . and living, I was dead.

Night-ride

Faster speed we through the bracken,
Catch me closer to your heart!
Clench the reins before they slacken
Lest the frightened filly start!
Oh, the blazing pennons whirling
Ruby jewels on the grass
And the burnished blossoms curling
Into phantoms as we pass!

Down the slender tongue of tracking
Let her fly, she cannot trip!
Back of us we hear the cracking
Of the scarlet stockman's whip.
He is rounding up his cattle —
Fiery steers and steeds of gold,
Crimson stallions — hear them rattle
Through the forest, fold on fold!

He is groaning with his plunder.
Turn her quickly to the creek!
Though his feet be swift as thunder
We shall hear his angry shriek
As we gallop, helter-skelter,
Through the cool and plashing tide,
To the land of peace and shelter
On the safe and southern side.

On he follows. Nearer, nearer
Ring his brumby's brazen feet.
Clipping-clopping, clearer, clearer —
Death's the fire we must defeat.
Keep your lips on mine, my darling,
Let the flame-flowers lick my hair;
Love can brook the angry snarling
Of their passionate despair.

Cross the creek—he cannot follow!
Love will ever conquer all.
Down we canter through the hollow
Safe at last from scathe and fall.

•

Thus I fancied we were speeding
All night long, with Love's control,
From our Passion and its pleading
To the safety of our soul.

Sonnets of Motherhood

XIX

Now all my senses have a double sense,
As this young life about my heart-fire sings,
Bringing to earth the everlasting things
God pours on woman as a recompense.
Great miracles of being, bright and tense,
Bloom from His garden of imaginings;
And long and deep, on happy seraph wings,
They fill my body with a dear suspense.

O blessed trinity of motherhood!
These tiny eyes unopened in me yet
Feed on the light of you, my spirit-spouse,
Through every marvel of each passing mood;
And in the passion of this wonder set
Our God Himself in holy travail bows.

XXXI

Belovèd, I who shall be mother soon
Need mothering myself this tired hour,
As heavily the sweet and precious power
Weighs on my heart till I am near to swoon.
Console me, soothe me, Dearest, with the boon
Of your firm strength, and little comforts shower
Soft on the drifting doubtings that devour
Patience and courage when the death-winds croon.

You are your mother, Dear, as I am mine.
And, as we slumber to our souls' caress,
Those two who panged for us and weeping smiled,
Draw near and bind us in a peace divine.
O mother me; all else is comfortless
As painted lips above a dying child.

Dulcie Deamer

Messalina

Cast back the doors!   I stifle!   Let the air
Of the outer night rush in and seize my hair
As with swift hands!   My slender body bare

Stretches, and sighs, and tautens like a thong . . . .
Oh, every hour of daylight does me wrong!
Why are the nights so brief, the days so long?

The days of mask-like faces, formalness,
Of downcast eyelid, pearl-entwisted tress;
I am the Emperor's wife: the ceilings press

Downward trap-fashion; rafters sheathed in gold
Are as cross-beams of pits that take and hold—
Tall pits of marble, glassy-smooth and cold.

I am the Emperor's wife . . . . I wore the hide
Of a she-leopard once; I rode the tide
Of splendid, savage seas, my glistening side

Compressed by triton-arms; I leapt and screamed
Where down the hill the naked Maenads streamed.
Beneath the droop of boughs, the faun's eyes gleamed

Goat-golden.   Oh, he found me where I lay!
I was a striving, but a laughing prey;
Crushed, conquered, wed—I knew not night or day.

Earth's unmixed passion gorges all my veins—
The scourging suns, the blinding summer rains,
The breast-white mountains and the panting plains.

What do I know of templed gods, and laws,
Honour, and duty?   All my essence draws
From older founts.   I see the clamped, stark jaws

Of rearing centaurs in their mating-fights;
The smell of blood and sweat and love delights
My widened nostrils.   Oh, those forest nights!—

The crying dark, the heavy blood-like dew,
The feet of Life and Death that both pursue,
The lusty, rank, insatiate satyr-crew . . .

I am the Emperor's wife—no! I am I!
The hot Earth bore me: though I live or die
I'll seek my old companions where they lie.

Stain both my lids with blue, my soles with red;
Sweeten with myrrh the black hair o'er me shed;
I will rise up and leave this empty bed.

A straight, thin, purple robe is all I'll wear;
I'll take no veil; unto my knees my hair
Falls.   Am I pale and burning?   Am I fair

As some lithe forest-thing with bloody lips?
Now—now to steal where the dark city dips
In reeking alleys, and the river slips . . .

My jungles!   Quick with lawless, fearless life;
The teeth of love, the death-fang of a knife,
And satyr-brawls, and Maenad-women's strife.

I'll enter by some strait, scarce-lighted door,
Cross with bare feet the dank and wine-wet floor—
Ah!   Now I am the Emperor's wife no more!

Swordsman, Greek boxer, Goth—they wait for me;
Now does my body live—now am I free!
My shredded robe slips downward to my knee . . . .

I am as naked as Life's naked flame!
None ever spoke of law or coward shame
In that spring-fevered world from which I came . . .
I fear no death.   Let swift sleep end the game!

The Young Martyr

I have just turned my fifteenth year
(My mother bore me at that age).
My name is Agatha.   A cage
Holds me: I have no fear.

(These simple things I must repeat
Over and over, lest my breath
Be stopped too soon by dazzling death,
Sun-gold from head to feet!)

I am a virgin.   On our wall
Was scratched the cross.   I sat within,
Hearing the laugh of hand-linked sin
And Saturnalia call.

Often they dashed their flowering boughs
Against our door.   Through one long chink
I saw them lift wreathed cups and drink,
Then, as a fair snake sloughs

Its diamond-patterned skin in spring
I saw a wild girl's sequined dress
Slip to her waist, and a mouth bless
Her breast, as babe-mouths cling.

My breast pained then.   But now it seems
As warmly full as though I fed
My first child there, and saw its head
Gleam as (they say) silk gleams.

To be caught up, bride-wise, to God,
To be all lost in Beauty—feel
Eternal arms, like thrice-forged steel,
And where great angels trod

Softly, slave-fashion, there to be
The proud belovéd!   Ah, caressed
By very Love! Clasped breast to breast,
God's close kiss known to me!

I shall quail then as though from flame,
Yet be as still as moulded snow
While waves of rapture come and go,
And God's Voice speaks my name—

The Voice that summoned day from night,
And called the mountains one by one
Up from the waters!   Ah, but none
Save I shall hear aright!

For uttered now for me alone
My name shall whisper through my hair
Like lovers' whispers . . . . Trumpets blare
Before a marble throne.

I hear the clang — the gates roll back.
Like pale, flat gold the circus-sand
Lies wide and void on either hand,
And zebra-striped with black

Three tigers move . . . . Divinest bliss
Slackens my knees.   How shall I meet
My Lover?   Oh, wine-reddened street
What were your joys to this?

Lesbia Harford

I can't feel the sunshine

I can't feel the sunshine
Or see the stars aright
For thinking of her beauty
And her kisses bright.

She would let me kiss her
Once and not again.
Deeming soul essential,
Sense doth she disdain.

If I should once kiss her,
I would never rest
Till I had lain hour long
Pillowed on her breast.

Lying so, I'd tell her
Many a secret thing
God has whispered to me
When my soul took wing.

Would that I were Sappho,
Greece my land, not this!
There the noblest women,
When they loved, would kiss.

Periodicity

My friend declares
Being woman and virgin she
Takes small account of periodicity

And she is right.
Her days are calmly spent
For her sex-function is irrelevant.

But I whose life
Is monthly broke in twain
Must seek some sort of meaning in my pain.

Women, I say,
Are beautiful in change,
Remote, immortal, like the moon they range.

Or call my pain
A skirmish in the whole
Tremendous conflict between body and soul.

Meaning must lie,
Some beauty surely dwell
In the fierce depths and uttermost pits of hell.

Yet still I seek,
Month after month in vain,
Meaning and beauty in recurrent pain.

Street Scene — Little Lonsdale St

I wish you'd seen that dirty little boy,
Finger at nose,
Peeking and ginking at some girls in rows
Seated on the high window-sills to rest.

One of the girls had hair as bright as corn.
And one was red.
And over their soft forms a glow was shed
From lamps new-lighted in the laundry there.

That boy, beneath them, wheeled a hand-cart full
Of cast-off busts
From sewing rooms. They looked like shells of lusts.
And all the girls around the windows laughed.

Pat wasn't Pat last night at all

Pat wasn't Pat last night at all.
He was the rain,
The Spring,
Young Dionysus, white and warm,
Lilac and everything.

Elsie Cole

Indictment

Mid-morn in the hills, and the golden air
    Brought honey and dew for breath;
The foot-track laughed to the sun, and there
    I saw the little black Death.

But Death had met Death in a stronger guise,
    And the slim black snake lay dead,
Broken and gashed, with his diamond eyes
    Crushed out of his battered head.

I looked at the terrible, innocent thing,
    The slayer savagely slain,
Till thought was mazed in its questioning
    And the sun was a mist of pain.

Searching and wondering, this I know:
    When the great Last Day is here
A cry in the dust from the whole world's foe
    That fires man's hate, through fear,

Will ring from many a mountain track
    To God, who plotted all ends,
Who gave, unasked for, the poison sac,
    Demanding amends, amends!

'Rickety Kate'

(Minnie Agnes Filson)

To the Main Roads Board

Leave me one road, an old road,
    Of red dust or brown,
A road that swings through singing gums
    Into some little town.

Leave me a road, a still road,
    Deep fringed with bracken and grass,
Where a man may walk and birds may play,
Fearless of things that pass.

Leave me a road, a brave road,
    Marked with incredible scars,
Where the scent of the dust is sweet in the rain,
    And small pools mirror stars.

Before Kosciusko

(After reading 'The Australian Alps')

I think if I had come
Into that shining gully
To the singing of the waters
Through tumbled russet rocks,
Where wattles were weighed down
With radiant buds of dew,
I think I would have followed
The long grey columns
Of gums indomitable
To where they halted, sensitive,

Not daring beyond the foot
Of that immaculate mountain.
Then I, too, would have stayed
And watched with them the sudden
Sacrilegious dawn
Climbing, gold and crimson,
Across the dazzling slopes
Till in that great white flame
All colour was engulfed
And utterly consumed.

•

I would have then turned back,
Remembering the dark
In the secret chasms of the mind,
And I would not have defiled
That high white country
With the sign of my ascending.
I would have been content
That my eyes had seen it.

Mary Finnin

Overtones on Australia Day

Set memory on the jar
For the ghosts
That slip through endlessly
(Eavesdrops from the overhang of time).

Speak carefully, you frogmouthed Robespierres,
For history overhears.

See how the tide laps strongly in the cove,
Swallowing the piled rocks and driven, feckless sands,
But carrying a boat's crew to these old, south lands . . .
Leichhardt dying greatly in the desert,
Companioned like a pharaoh by friends, and beasts, and gear;
The heart of Kennedy choked in spear-stopped blood;
A woman giving birth in the bough shade;
Under the sweating sun by the mountain road
A man in irons munching salted beef;
A young soldier falling in lead rain before Gallipoli Heights;
And also, on this day,
The one who stayed his woomera at Botany Bay.

The Farm Near Norman's Lane

That old man at the farm near Norman's Lane,
(Wormwood and horehound winding all the way)—
Waits for his sons to change,
For times to come again
To the hard row
His father had to hoe.

(Show them what's what, he thinks,
The old man marking time at the wicket gate;
And best of all, not worry him a bit,
Snug sandwiched in life's troubles
Like bread about salt meat.)

Niggard as noonday shade,
He stands at the wicket gate—
A break in the gorse hedge flowing
Over its lurking shadow.

'Times are too good; but still 'n all
Them terriers have the mange,
(They catch it from the foxes on the hill);
Kero and mutton fat's the stuff;
I'll mix it soon;
Soon as ye've gone.
But wait in the sun.

'A man in armour now—
You'd fix him with a drop of oil at the joints;
But my old woman stiffens in her bed;
And medicine don't do a mite of good.'

He has dressed the soil to rape it over again.
His features, carved to petulance, endure.
His nose divides the wind, his eyes
Smoulder in caves of darkness,
As he fronts the sea beyond his boundaries.
Far more
Than the skylarks to show for his sixty years:

A scratch-bright car; all fences strained and strong;
And three spoilt sons to brawl with all day long;
That girl too smart for her own good, wanting the best;
Wife wading through pain to an isle of painless rest.

But skylarks poise, like Simeon Stylites;
Standing on air, they sing
Of capeweed spread for one long, yellow day.
Tomorrow will beat up an easterly swell,
Flood the sea marsh, salt down another spring.

Winter Upland

The granite boulder on the rise
Cuts midnight clear
From moonset in the highlands,
From the morning star.

Frost hardens on the fleece
Like long-remembered words;
Bark slivers on the boxwood
Become white swords.

Now, calm for her moment,
Ewe waits beneath the stone
To deliver life that beats
Upon dim gates of pain.

But a lamb's breath will not steam
Upon that starlit air;
For, busy as a midwife,
An old red fox is there.

Dorothy Drain

Christmas, they say

Christmas, they say, should be white, with the holly growing
Scarlet and green against the sleeping garden,
And the snow falling, falling, mantling the eaves and wrapping
Each hearth in its magic circle of home.

So they dreamed of home, the expatriates, lonely, not knowing
That they carried in their hearts not snow, nor robins, nor holly,
But the age old wish for belonging.

Ours is a golden Christmas, cicadas shrilling,
Golden and blue, with the long waves rolling, rolling,
The still grey trees of the bush in the noonday silence,
The blistered roads of the city, the blue hydrangea
Bright in the sun around the suburban portals.

And this is the dream that our children's children will carry,
For Christmas lives in the heart, and this is our own.

Elizabeth Riddell

News of a Baby

Welcome, baby, to the world of swords
And deadlier words.
We offer you a rough bed, and tears at morning,
And soon a playground
Bounded by ice and stones,
A buttonhole of thorns,
A kiss on war's corner.

We promise you, baby,
The stumble of fear in the heart,
The lurch of fear in the bones.

Painted upon your mother's cheek already
I see the dark effusion of your blood,
Bending already beside her patient chair the bandaged ghosts.
Welcome, baby, no dread thing will be omitted.
We are your eager hosts.

To Stay Alive

To stay alive
(I am reminded by one who is alive
and kicking against the pricks,
no pun intended)
I should speak to seven people every day.

I should also touch the round head of a cat,
rasp an orange skin, buy bread,
walk on grass, write a postcard.
That's to stay alive.

Such endeavours should be chosen thoughtfully, he says,
Collecting pine cones in the park I must
observe the little hidden frontiers where the sedge
marches with water hyacinth
and study the sacred ibis, how it steps
carefully in the shallows.

To stay alive, he says, avoid monotony,
keep a diary, every night identify a star
(that's not monotonous?)
but above all speak to seven people
who will not confuse me.

Only the telephone will confuse me
when the wrong voice offers the right advice
I do not wish to hear.

The Time of Life

I owned my body once but now my body owns me.
It bends me, breaks me,
gnarls my fingers, splits my nails,
paints me in red and grey and brown,
splinters my bones, shreds my skin,
leaches the colour from my lips and eyes.

My body tells me what to do and why
where once I gave the orders—love here, love there.
The takeover was a slow affair,
painful, it diminished me,
but I can say now all is over.
The crying is finished with the kissing. All is quiet
except for a little late rebellious heat,
a random pang of memory in the blood.

Here Lies

Weep, if ever you have wept, for this beautiful youth . . .
he was on his way to a café when a prostitute shot him.
            Inscription on a tomb on an island in the Aegean Sea

The lies they set on tombstones live and lie
Forever in cold stone. The way they tell it
He was pure gold, perfect flower of men

Who, wearing his second-best suit and carrying figs
To stop his hunger, went to drink some wine
And play backgammon with other village heroes
Outside the café, in the cypressed dusk.

And was shot. Astonished, he turned then
And offered his hand to the girl
With the gun, and stumbled and died.

What a tragedy, said the gossips
Into their black kerchiefs.
But the stonepines and the swifts
Tell another story.
'She was a good and lovely girl and he betrayed her,
The cockerel, with promises.
So this poor girl (no whore)
Shot him to avenge her honour,
And for all thin girls with big eyes
Who have been robbed of laughter
(For it has happened before).'

Finally she was invited in marriage
By the man who kept the café,
And lived happily ever after
Though avoiding the graveyard
When she walked out at sunset.

The most terrible of all lies
Are those set out with love
Under the weeping angel, the cross and the crouched dove,
On cold stone.

Margaret Diesendorf

the grey man

he controls my life   when i wake he stands by my bed
fully dressed shirt & tie   the eyes the now familiar
stare through unfashionable spectacles   i look at
his large mouth with the too regular teeth & wish he'd
come to bed   he reads my suggestive gaze & shakes his
head   lord   the wrong time again he's off to work with no
thought of sex   yet i know only too well that when *he*
finds it the right time he can be quite passionate   he

vanishes into the bedroom door   i feel desperate . . .
deserted alone   he won't come back i fear   i get
up & dress   drink my coffee & eat my toast   take the
prescribed vitamin pills & try to settle down to
work forgetting my chronic ills   i've typed about a
thousand words when i'm forced to look up: a shadow falls
across the page: he's back: i sink into his fleshless
arms & they squeeze tighter than flesh   his eyes turn green   it's
the wrong time i murmur   but he does not reply   we
are somewhere out at sea   on water   i'm not sure where
i begin where i end   where i'm from   am i alone
or are we two   when is lie what is true   my body
smiles a moon-glut smile   all in this world is right   nothing
is wrong   when i open my eyes he's gone is gone . . . i
start to bleed from an unseen wound   i call but there's no
more response   back to the typewriter back to the text
this can't go on . . . i now draft quietly & undisturbed
he's back to his magic country his desire quenched he's
forgotten about love . . . i also need to forget
so decide to go out   as i walk in the street   i
suddenly sense the grey man is right inside me   i
burn like a log on fire   my legs stiffen   i can't move

To break my solitude

To break my solitude
I look into the glass:
     Good day, my honest friend,
more honest than my shadow . . .
What's that? Despair
today stares
out of your eyes.
          Come,
smile: you are not alone,
you have company,
I am home.
Perhaps I should,
in my present state
of lovelessness,
put mirrors all
around
as they did in Vienna's Imperial
Town Hall

where as a student
I danced the quadrille . . .
stepping in & out
of the rhythmic square
for *pantalon, été, poule,*
pastourelle, finale.
Perhaps I should
change my room
into a mirrored hall,
people it with Margarets,
the many Margarets
(smiling, laughing, shouting,
screaming, kow-towing,
scowling, spitting, hissing
at each other . . . shamming)
the many Margarets
you said
I am.

Only the gods can hear the moan

Only the gods can hear the moan
of the cells
once pain has transcended
its own threshold
& the iron curtain
of silence
fallen across the victim's mouth—
like diving down
to an evil sea,
to a soundless region:
now the memories of love
swim past one another indifferently
without nodding
(amazed at the change of habitat),
species as diverse as
blue demoiselle & seahorse,
lion fish & sea dragon;
moorish idols pour the light
of their brilliant colours
into the black velvet;
others

wrapped in pearl-grey veils
no longer count their losses,
ghostlike world
where only phosphorescent flashes
intimate
to the uninvolved
in the sunlit coastal
waters
that here
death is not yet final . . .

Barbara Giles

Reading an Erotic Novel at a Late Age

The little wild strawberries are good to eat,
so are Norwegian herrings, buttermilk potatoes
and the apple pie we had Tuesday.
In memories of memories of pleasure
the taste will not come back, the mouth won't water.

Offer me strawberries, I'll cry, 'Delicious,'
pour cream on apple pie, I smack my lips.
I smell the roast, I've got an appetite.

And I remember all that ravenous loving.
Offer me love, I'll fob you off with kisses.

A Careful Childhood

In my parents' house there was
no Bluebeard chamber, no
cupboard drawer but was
orderly, uncrowded, open.
No scarlet drops, no tangled
hunks of hair on our shining
floors, though safely hidden
under the knickers, the cambric
petticoats, lay Marie Stopes.

The cabin trunks were empty
in the shed. Secrets
were locked in flesh.
Sometimes my father,
silent and sulking
made his bed in the hay.

Voices never were raised. Lightnings
flickered, one could never have called it
peace. How did I become so furious
unless for that anger, exemplary,
never unleashed.

Mama's Little Girl

An unlucky year
in a strange city
with a crazed husband
when you, my little girl,
said you were coming.

The house looked respectable.
In another room
someone was playing Mozart.
'Just grit your teeth.' And after
I walked soft-legged out,
having put off your visit
permanently, little one.

With better times, tall sons.

In iron-hard necessity I left you
upon the mountain for the bears to take.
A kind of logic says she was our daughter.

Vera Newsom

Midnight Snow

That wind has many voices: women
who walk alone listen for a lull in the storm
to piece the words together, but it's only
when wind thrashes the eucalypts
they hear the voices, on the gully's edge.
Careful. A gust could snap the branches,
fling them over the precipice. It's always
at the breaking point they hear them,
like kites bucking against their strings
to be snatched away by a shift in the wind.
Voices, whispering of the cliff's edge,
breasts' declivities, laughter,
the sharp spears of fire. Midnight snow.

•

You were laughing
straight in my eyes, your hands on my shoulders,
bone pressing bone. Then they slid to my breasts.
Quick as spring buds I could feel them rising.
Outside, there was snow. We could tell by the silence.
You piled on more logs till the flames leaping higher
reached their crescendo. Later,
we banked down the fire. All winter,
we had fuel, and to spare.

•

What are you saying?
There was a gale and the eucalypts whining
threw down dead wood. All our lives
we'd walked on the cliffedge, no thought of slipping.
Then, foothold uncertain, bones paper bark thin,
it was 'any time, now' . . .

•

It's strange,
when hot sun flattens the landscape
I never hear your voice; but should the wind rise
or the moon make midnight shadows on the snow
you are most real. To love is to be vulnerable.
I do not grudge the risk, would choose again
to walk on the precipice edge.

Judith Wright

Woman to Man

The eyeless labourer in the night,
the selfless, shapeless seed I hold,
builds for its resurrection day—
silent and swift and deep from sight
foresees the unimagined light.

This is no child with a child's face;
this has no name to name it by;
yet you and I have known it well.
This is our hunter and our chase,
the third who lay in our embrace.

This is the strength that your arm knows,
the arc of flesh that is my breast,
the precise crystals of our eyes.
This is the blood's wild tree that grows
the intricate and folded rose.

This is the maker and the made;
this is the question and reply;
the blind head butting at the dark,
the blaze of light along the blade.
Oh hold me, for I am afraid.

At Cooloolah

The blue crane fishing in Cooloolah's twilight
has fished there longer than our centuries.
He is the certain heir of lake and evening,
and he will wear their colour till he dies;

but I'm a stranger, come of a conquering people.
I cannot share his calm, who watch his lake,
being unloved by all my eyes delight in
and made uneasy, for an old murder's sake.

Those dark-skinned people who once named Cooloolah
knew that no land is lost or won by wars,
for earth is spirit; the invader's feet will tangle
in nets there and his blood be thinned by fears.

Riding at noon and ninety years ago,
my grandfather was beckoned by a ghost—
a black accoutred warrior armed for fighting,
who sank into bare plain, as now into time past.

White shores of sand, plumed reed and paperbark,
clear heavenly levels frequented by crane and swan—
I know that we are justified only by love,
but oppressed by arrogant guilt, have room for none.

And walking on clean sand among the prints
of bird and animal, I am challenged by a driftwood spear
thrust from the water; and, like my grandfather,
must quiet a heart accused by its own fear.

To Another Housewife

Do you remember how we went,
on duty bound, to feed the crowd
of hungry dogs your father kept
as rabbit-hunters? Lean and loud,
half-starved and furious, how they leapt
against their chains, as though they meant
in mindless rage for being fed,
to tear our childish hands instead!

With tomahawk and knife we hacked
the flyblown tatters of old meat,
gagged at their carcass-smell, and threw
the scraps and watched the hungry eat.
Then turning faint, we made a pact,
(two greensick girls), crossed hearts and swore
to touch no meat forever more.

How many cuts of choice and prime
our housewife hands have dressed since then—
these hands with love and blood imbrued—
for daughters, sons, and hungry men!
How many creatures bred for food
we've raised and fattened for the time
they met at last the steaming knife
that serves the feast of death-in-life!

And as the evening meal is served
we hear the turned-down radio
begin to tell the evening news
just as the family joint is carved.
O murder, famine, pious wars . . .
Our children shrink to see us so,
in sudden meditation, stand
with knife and fork in either hand.

Request to a Year

If the year is meditating a suitable gift,
I should like it to be the attitude
of my great-great-grandmother,
legendary devotee of the arts,

who, having had eight children
and little opportunity for painting pictures,
sat one day on a high rock
beside a river in Switzerland,

and from a difficult distance viewed
her second son, balanced on a small ice-floe,
drift down the current towards a waterfall
that struck rock-bottom eighty feet below,

while her second daughter, impeded,
no doubt, by the petticoats of the day,
stretched out a last-hope alpenstock
(which luckily later caught him on his way).

Nothing, it was evident, could be done;
and with the artist's isolating eye
my great-great-grandmother hastily sketched the scene.
The sketch survives to prove the story by.

Year, if you have no Mother's Day present planned,
reach back and bring me the firmness of her hand.

Australia 1970

Die, wild country, like the eaglehawk,
dangerous till the last breath's gone,
clawing and striking. Die
cursing your captor through a raging eye.

Die like the tigersnake
that hisses such pure hatred from its pain
as fills the killer's dreams
with fear like suicide's invading stain.

Suffer, wild country, like the ironwood
that gaps the dozer-blade.
I see your living soil ebb with the tree
to naked poverty.

Die like the soldier-ant
mindless and faithful to your million years.
Though we corrupt you with our torturing mind,
stay obstinate; stay blind.

For we are conquerors and self-poisoners
more than scorpion or snake
and dying of the venoms that we make
even while you die of us.

I praise the scoring drought, the flying dust,
the drying creek, the furious animal,
that they oppose us still;
that we are ruined by the thing we kill.

Wedding Photograph, 1913

Ineloquent, side by side, this country couple
smiling confettied outside the family house—
he with his awkward faun-look, ears spread wide,
she with her downward conscious poise of beauty;
surrounded, wished-for, toasted by your clans
in the last threatening calm before the wars—
I look at you and wonder if I knew you.

Fathers and mothers enter an old pattern,
whoever they are; assume it for the children's
dependent and rebellious eyes. I see you
not through this amateur happy snapshot's sepias
but through the smell of a tweed shoulder sobbed-on,
through picnics, scoldings, moralities imparted
shyly, the sound of songs at a piano—

through all I had to learn and to unlearn,
absorb and fight against; through tears, then, better
remembered than through your love and kindnesses.
And she, pointing out birds or pansies' eyebrows,
gentle, fighting increasing pain—I know her
better from this averted girlish face
than in those memories death cut so short.

That was the most important thing she showed us—
that pain increases, death is final,
that people vanish. She never thought of that,
her second bridegroom, standing there invisible
at her right hand. Nor he of grief
whose laughing easy look was furrowed later
by private and public matters. He lived long—

so long, I knew him well. Or so I thought;
but now I wonder. Here in this photograph
stand two whom I can ponder. Let me join

that happy crowd of cousins, sisters, parents,
brothers and friends. I lift a glass as well—
the grey-haired daughter whom you did not know.
The best of luck, young darlings.
Go on your honeymoon. Be happy always.

For a Pastoral Family

1   To my brothers

Over the years, horses have changed to land-rovers.
Grown old, you travel your thousands of acres
deploring change and the wickedness of cities
and the cities' politics: hoping to pass to your sons
a kind of life you inherited in your generation.

Some actions of those you vote for stick in your throats.
There are corruptions one cannot quite endorse;
but if they are in our interests, then of course . . .

Well, there are luxuries still,
including pastoral silence, miles of slope and hill,
the cautious politeness of bankers. These are owed
to the forerunners, men and women
who took over as if by right a century and a half
in an ancient difficult bush. And after all,
the previous owners put up little fight,
did not believe in ownership, and so were scarcely human.

Our people who gnawed at the fringe
of the edible leaf of this country
left you a margin of action, a rural security,
and left to me
what serves as a base for poetry,
a doubtful song that has a dying fall.

2   *To my generation*

A certain consensus of echo, a sanctioning sound,
supported our childhood lives. We stepped
on sure and conceded ground.
A whole society
extended a comforting cover of legality.
The really deplorable deeds
had happened out of our sight, allowing us innocence,
We were not born, or there was silence kept.

If now there are landslides, if our field of reference
is much eroded, our hands show little blood.
We enter a plea: Not Guilty.
For the good of the Old Country
the land was taken; the Empire had loyal service.
Would any convict us?
Our plea has been endorsed by every appropriate jury.

If my poetic style, your pastoral produce,
are challenged by shifts in the market,
or a change of taste, at least we can go down smiling
with enough left in our pockets
to be noted in literary or local histories.

3   *For today*

We were always part of a process. It has expanded.
What swells over us now is a logical spread
from the small horizons we made—
the heave of the great corporations
whose bellies are never full.
What sort of takeover bid
could you knock back now if the miners,
the junk-food firms or their processors want your land?
Or worse, leave you alone to hoe
small beans in a dwindling row?

The fears of our great-grandfathers—
apart from a fall in the English market—
were of spearwood, stone axes. Sleeping
they sprang awake at the crack
of frost on the roof, the yawn and stretching
of a slab wall. We turn on the radio
for news from the USA or USSR
against which no comfort or hope
might come from the cattle prizes at the Show.

4   *Pastoral lives*

Yet a marginal sort of grace
as I remember it, softened our arrogant clan.
We were fairly kind to horses
and to people not too different from ourselves.
Kipling and A.A. Milne were our favourite authors
but Shelley, Tennyson, Shakespeare stood on our shelves—
suitable reading for women,
to whom, after all, the amenities had to be left.

An undiscursive lot (discourse is for the city)
one of us helped to found a university.
We respected wit in others,
though we kept our own for weddings,
unsure of the *bona fides* of the witty.

In England, we called on relatives,
assuming welcome for the sake of a shared bloodline,
but kept our independence.
We would entertain them equally, if they came,

and with equal hospitality—
blood being thicker than thousands of miles of waters—
for the sake of Great-aunt Charlotte and old letters.

At church, the truncate inarticulate
Anglican half-confession
'there is no health in us'
made us gag a little. We knew we had no betters
though too many were worse.
We passed on the collection-plate
adding a reasonable donation.

That God approved us was obvious.
Most of our ventures were prosperous.
As for the *Dies Irae*
we would deal with that when we came to it.

5   *Change*

At best, the men of our clan
have been, or might have been,
like Yeats' fisherman.
A small stream, narrow but clean,

running apart from the world.
Those hills might keep them so,
granite, gentle and cold.
But hills erode, streams go

through settlement and town
darkened by chemical silt.
Dams hold and slow them down,
trade thickens them like guilt.

All men grow evil with trade
as all roads lead to the city.
Willie Yeats would have said,
perhaps, the more the pity.

But how can we be sure?
Wasn't his chosen man
as ignorant as pure?
Keep out? Stay clean? Who can?

6   *Kinship*

Blue early mist in the valley. Apricots
bowing the orchard-trees, flushed red with summer,
loading bronze-plaqued branches;
our teeth in those sweet buttock-curves. Remember
the horses swinging to the yards, the smell
of cattle, sweat and saddle-leather?
Blue ranges underlined the sky. In any weather
it was well, being young and simple,
letting the horses canter home together.

All those sights, smells and sounds we shared
trailing behind grey sheep, red cattle,
from Two-rail or Ponds Creek
through tawny pastures breathing pennyroyal.
In winter, sleety winds bit hands and locked
fingers round reins. In spring, the wattle.

With so much past in common,
on the whole we forgive each other
for the ways in which we differ—
two old men, one older woman.
When one of us falls ill,
the others may think less
of today's person, the lined and guarding face,

than of a barefoot child running careless through
long grass where snakes lie, or forgetting
to watch in the paddocks for the black Jersey bull.
Divisions and gulfs deepen
daily, the world over,
more dangerously than now between us three.
Which is why, while there is time (though not our form at all)
I put the memories into poetry.

Dorothy Auchterlonie

A Problem of Language

How praise a man? She cannot vow
His lips are red, his brow is snow,
Nor celebrate a smooth white breast
While gazing on his hairy chest;
And though a well-turned leg might please,

More often he has knobbly knees;
His hair excites no rapt attention—
If there's enough of it to mention.
She cannot praise his damask skin,
Still less the suit he's wrapped it in;
And even if he's like Apollo
To gaze upon, it does not follow
That she may specify the features
That mark him off from other creatures.
No rime can hymn her great occasion
But by a process of evasion;
And so she gives the problem over,
Describes her love, but not her lover,
Despairs of words to tell us that
Her heart sings his magnificat.

Helen Haenke

Motel Dining-room

What is he doing, the great god Pan,
piping music like whipped cream
around the edge of every dish?
  I'll be loving you, always,
sharper than salt in the consomme
and mustard on the beef.
And why, O Pan, do I eat the parfait here
that I could not buy in my sixteenth year?
Again I—*were the only girl in the world*
and Mantovani the boy beyond my coffee.
I waltz in smalzy metaphors for arms
with lads of nineteen-thirty-two
who made *me a part of the song in their heart.*

All by myself, not *in the moonlight*
but a fluorescent glare tearing strips off my
rose-coloured tablecloth
with fake-fruit centre-piece.

At separate tables, three men like my brothers,
sit staring at the same harvest.
We seem careful not to rattle spoons in empty cups.

Pear Tree

When I reached the little valley, as you said
there was nothing but a pear tree curdled with bloom.
At the motel last night, you said
you drove through by mistake and what a sight!
You did not stop—why stop? You'd seen it.

In Japan, a poet walked his failing years
a hundred miles of robbers, floods and mountain ice
to see a plum tree. He did not say what he did
there, but he wrote three lines of poetry
to last three hundred years: the tree alone sufficient
for his poem. But I search back to the seed and see

the pile of rubbled chimney-bricks beneath the turf
the stone door-step jutting up, the row of pine stumps
leading to the creek—so the wind blows westerly?—
and arums, green as oceans, clumping in the soak.

I see the woman, wrapping her red hands
in a blackstuff apron, and calling a stop to work
and her man to 'See the tree!' and their children—
freckled, squinting through the sun—hand-in-hand
between them, all knowing the moment's poem.

No one wrote the blossom or the veil of bees
or the white petals falling in no-wind or the humming
or the butcher-bird praising his dinner with snatches
of insects and Rachmaninoff. No one knew—
thinking of pear-juice running down their chins
and jam, preserves and chutney, to eat summer
at their winter board; and in the winter no one thought
of this blossom-day, so sure it comes again—no one knew

they would all be one with pears and quinces, roses,
spindly palms and apples, lemons, wide-armed figs,
and elm and poplar spinneys standing lost
in sudden clearings all over the country
to mark some living place.

Nancy Cato

River Scene

Slowly rose the crane, blue crane . . .
Long legs idly drooping,
Sweep of wings, curve
Cutting the sky arclike. Again
Above the river,
Green slow lethargic river,
Lazily
He circles once, and now
With careless dignity
Sweeps out across the plain.

Unseen
The reed-warbler babbles in that clump of sedge,
While little lizards, leaf-marked grey and brown,
Pause by a fallen log
Or slip to the water's edge.
Limp in the sun
Long-leaved, the coolibahs are drooped.
Slow windmills turn
High on the yellow sandstone cliff.
White sands burn
The shrinking feet;
The river drowses, tired and still with heat.

The Lovers

An hour those cloudy lovers lay embraced
Above the purple hill, in the blue sky:
Her face upturned, and shadowed dark by his.
The sun streamed down in glory on his hair,
White-gold in the warm light, and on her rich
And snowy curves. They seemed a god-like pair,
And formed for some immortal, endless bliss.

Yet, when the sun sank westward, they were gone,
—Ravelled by winds and strewn across the sky,
And in their place had moved a thousand forms
Of dog and ape and bear, though the dark thrust
Of hills, and blue of sky, were still unchanged;
Like any mortal lovers turned to dust,
And driven before the breath of coming storms.

Mallee Farmer

You planted wheat and you reaped white gibbers
You ran some sheep but the crows were robbers
Of eyes and entrails and even the wool,
Plucked from the carcass before it was cool.

You cleared the mallee and sand blew over
Fence and road to the slow green river,
You prayed for rain but the sky breathed dust
Of long-dead farmers and the soil's red rust.

You ploughed up the paddocks with a stump-jump plough,
But the gates were open and the drought walked through:
Now the old house crumbles and bares its bones
And the land is left to the crows and the stones.

Anne Elder

School Cadets

The day of the fête—and what a day for it,
blazing with *bonhomie* and sun. But what a fate
for the dads jam-packed in the hoop-la tent; for Mum
buying back the cakes she sent. The mike
crackles amicably: Your presence is requested,
Ladies and Gentlemen, on the lower field.
'Crikey what a row!' the juniors bawl.
'Only the old Cadets—can't march for nuts!'
But Colonel Bogey, limping a bit, but still
incorruptible, taking fair advantage
of the British Raj and The Bridge on the River Kwai,
draws them by the nose. The chins go up
on the kid sisters, bearded in fairy-floss.
                         Formidable Headmaster,
affecting a walking stick, conversing precisely,
escorts the Mayoress to see how nicely
the Best School teaches the game of War.

They wheel on the green glare of grass
like stripling gods in cohort, and stars
are struck from their brass, the moving frieze
of their bright lives unrolls. The gaiters surge
and ripple as a white wave of the sea.
The tune blurts out and strangles, faltering
to slow march half a tone off key.

'Excuse me—excuse me'—the mothers are shoving
like hooligans. There he is! The short one, third
from the right, sloped in the tango embrace
of the great spiralled horn. Impossible to separate
that agonising familiar forlorn
lowing practised in bathrooms on holiday.

He is pitiful
as a babe in python coils, they are pitiful
all of them, they are terrible
as Kings in Babylon. The hateful nations
inhabit their slight frames, and future leers
desirous on their wavering formations.
Earnestly they are inflated, diminished . . . and *away* . . .

The Bachelor

There was an old friend through all our childhood
who walked with my father, reliving the batching days
of cream flannels and the nicest girls in Perth
with pink pomade complexions that still warmed
his memory. I could hear the tea-sets tinkle,
the laughter from basket chairs with the racquets flung
on the lawn. I listened to the sunny past
or tales of the War, or the greatest old Tests replayed
in the ritual tones you would keep for poems;
and as I grew he was part of the family air.

He was the classic bachelor, almost a freak
of plainness with a great bony Scottish nose
and a mouth like the jaw of a dog that hinged
on a bark of laughter or set in abysmal gloom
until an ephemeral sweetness played
in response to some whim or humour. Above all, shy.
But masculine, rangy, gallant in baggy tweed,
someone between a laird and a leprechaun
who panicked at strangers, vanishing by the back door
in a puff of smoke with runic mutterings.

Trained in the Law, he couldn't abide his desk
after the soldiering and became that denizen
of *pensions* whose modest private means
are just enough to keep him wandering
contentedly from Nice to Switzerland
and over to Lords for the matches and off
again to Damascus or soft South Seas.
Under his battered panama or cap
elusive and unfashionable he browsed
through marvels and found reluctantly
that he was a little poor and a little tired.

So back at last to rent a room in Melbourne
close to the parks where he sauntered head in air
snuffing the morning and bending his large nose
to some great friend of flower or tree.
Weather inclement, he sat at home in a muffler,
careful of health, and tidied over his store
of books, of prints from the Louvre, Greek friezes,
or tinted his snapshots of the Côte d'Azur;
and sometimes took a tram to the galleries, lunched
on a munch of raisins and saved for the next trip.

January: he put up his nose and took
the lure of the sea, and graced our holidays
with a gentle sparkle; truly the heart and soul
of the boarding house, bowing to maiden ladies
(or cutting them dead with inscrutable modesty
on the way to the bath) and giving
his wobbly seascapes bashfully away.
He sprouted cap and bells, was a daring jester,
a peddler of spells and a fossicker of the tide
who carried wonders carefully home for children
and turned a broken shell to a fairytale.

A wedding: Miraculously he consented
to speechify, rose tall to the occasion
and brought down the house with a turn of fanciful wit
and then, a little pink with success and cocktails
left suddenly for the haven of his cold room
to sup frugally on the laughter of friends.

He'd grown a little mad perhaps; soliloquized
at windows, expelling a loud guffaw
in an empty room—but all dreamers do that
and the lonely—it is no fault.

And so he mooched and mooned and lost
his appetite for food and friends and trees.
All weather menaced him with imagined chill
and he lay sick, in mortal terror of nurses
and turned a lugubrious cheekbone to the wall.

He died in a hospital for old soldiers,
unable to meet the mateship from the next bed.
He'd shied from my visit. I took him a prime rose
called The Doctor, lemon-scented, much too late.
Once a great one for the scents and the apt names
he needed prayers now and a strong cradling arm.
But how he would have hated them! He knew
he was done for, cast in ignominy. I saw
the old smile deprecate its own despair.

The rose trembles, rejected for eternity.
I failed him and for this was to have the pain
of reward—to make my entranced choice
of his queer treasures and to read
his poems, at worst innocuous whimsy, at best
a naked dereliction till then inviolate.
And one of the worst to me, a pointed girl
poised on the brink of a pool which of course was Life.
It was a light quip with classical allusions.
He was a good trier, dogged by imperfections
and all my understanding goes to him
saying: I have caught the glimpse and am satisfied.

He shaped me more than he knew with the delicate finger
of eccentricity. His beautiful gifts
of a yellow plate or a misty lithograph
or a cobweb chain of topaz dewdrops
coiled in an old box, fed me an odd taste
for the flower a little beyond the pale.
No one knew him well—he was too raw
for the staggering immodesty of love. We loved him
with distant tact. But as the distance dwindles
between my garrulous present and the huge
reticence which we must share at last
his pure worth comes to me, a gem
I startled from the crusty rock of habit,
an aquamarine like his sea-loving eye.

And reading his verses sometimes to confirm
affection, I see him walking thin and slow
and absent, searching his spirit for the line
of touching power he almost found, and wish
profoundly I were better skilled, and not so late
to run up warmly to his shoulder and say: 'Jim!
I've just found this—is it yours or mine?'

At Haworth

A name: incongruously mild
and maidenly, blown to me
across an exact century from birth
to birth too late for meeting.
But these are the moors
met at last and not misleading.
Still dark gold, I tell you, bronze
in the wind, high in the dark wind of evening
that plucks away a voice, a feather,
so that asking how you are faring
I catch at down . . .
you took them, the visitant pinions
that came at you once, twice, fierce,
awaited in the hour of stars
over the moors.

The narrow house: that some have seen
as morbid damp (*I* could move in
tomorrow, except it is full)—a strict frame
with the right smell of a close family;
and the smallest room in the world
where the hard bright crown of fame
and of the vision's forewarning
shone as a betrothal-ring heaven-sent
to the prison that was haven. In secret,
stubborn and plain, you practised to wear it:
to stand alone, curb the tongue,
rise early, look daily at graves,
set the lit word in cryptic by a dying wick,
meet the last hour in a neat dress,
hair parted dead centre, and,
upright on a tight horsehair settee
choke on rattling blood with such asperity.

But a door: a gate, a worn path climbing
up to escape, to some kind of sharp
ambiguous meeting—granted, in the moor air
it's a white girl again, walking,
a wild sprig tucked at the breast for safekeeping
against the black bronze wind. Then ravening
like a she-werewolf at the barred window
for love, affinity, the lust of the consuming
spirit unrequited—wear it like a hard crown,
bear it, will it down
on the blown wings of moorland birds returning
to known high lands at evening

Emily
look, I am kneeling
sawing my wrists on the broken glass
of this stammering spring . . .
and on the words, in envy.

Rosemary Dobson

In a Café

She clasps the cup with both her hands,
Over the rim her glance compels
(A man forgets his hat, returns,
The waitress leans against the shelves).

And Botticelli, painting in the corner,
Glances absorbed across a half-turned shoulder
Thinking of lilies springing where she walks
As now she rises, moves across the room,
(The yawning waitress gathers up the stalks,
The ash, the butt-ends and the dregs of tea).
Pausing between the gesture and the motion,
Lifting her hand to brush away her hair,
He limns her in an instant, always there
Between the doorway and the emphatic till
With waves and angels, balanced on a shell.

The Bystander

I am the one who looks the other way,
In any painting you may see me stand
Rapt at the sky, a bird, an angel's wing,
While others kneel, present the myrrh, receive
The benediction from the radiant hand.

I hold the horses while the knights dismount
And draw their swords to fight the battle out;
Or else in dim perspective you may see
My distant figure on the mountain road
When in the plains the hosts are put to rout.

I am the silly soul who looks too late,
The dullard dreaming, second from the right.
I hang upon the crowd, but do not mark
(Cap over eyes) the slaughtered Innocents,
Or Icarus, his downward-plunging flight.

Once in a Garden—back view only there—
How well the painter placed me, stroke on stroke,
Yet scarcely seen among the flowers and grass—
I heard a voice say, 'Eat,' and would have turned—
I often wonder who it was that spoke.

Child with a Cockatoo

Portrait of Anne, daughter of the Earl of Bedford, by S. Verelst

'Paid by my lord, one portrait, Lady Anne,
Full length with bird and landscape, twenty pounds
And framed withal. I say received. Verelst.'

So signed the painter, bowed, and took his leave.
My Lady Anne smiled in the gallery
A small, grave child, dark-eyed, half turned to show
Her five bare toes beneath the garment's hem,
In stormy landscape with a swirl of drapes.
And, who knows why, perhaps my lady wept
To stand so long and watch the painter's brush
Flicker between the palette and the cloth
While from the sun-drenched orchard all the day
She heard her sisters calling each to each.

And someone gave, to drive the tears away,
That sulphur-crested bird with great white wings,
The wise, harsh bird—as old and wise as Time
Whose well-dark eyes the wonder kept and closed.
So many years to come and still, he knew,
Brooded that great, dark island continent
Terra Australis.
                            To those fabled shores
Not William Dampier, pirating for gold,
Nor Captain Cook his westward course had set
Jumped from the longboat, waded through the surf,
And clapt his flag ashore at Botany Bay.
Terra Australis, unimagined land—
Only that sulphur-crested bird could tell
Of dark men moving silently through trees,
Of stones and silent dawns, of blackened earth
And the long golden blaze of afternoon.
That vagrant which an ear-ringed sailor caught
(Dropped from the sky, near dead, far out to sea)
And caged and kept, till, landing at the docks,
Walked whistling up the Strand and sold it then,
The curious bird, its cynic eyes half closed,
To the Duke's steward, drunken at an inn.
And he lived on, the old adventurer,
And kept his counsel, was a sign unread,
A disregarded prologue to an age.
So one might find a meteor from the sun
Or sound one trumpet ere the play's begun.

Cock Crow

Wanting to be myself, alone,
Between the lit house and the town
I took the road, and at the bridge
Turned back and walked the way I'd come.

Three times I took that lonely stretch,
Three times the dark trees closed me round,
The night absolved me of my bonds
Only my footsteps held the ground.

My mother and my daughter slept,
One life behind and one before,
And I that stood between denied
Their needs in shutting-to the door.

And walking up and down the road
Knew myself, separate and alone,
Cut off from human cries, from pain,
And love that grows about the bone.

Too brief illusion! Thrice for me
I heard the cock crow on the hill,
And turned the handle of the door
Thinking I knew his meaning well.

The Three Fates

At the instant of drowning he invoked the three sisters.
It was a mistake, an aberration, to cry out for
Life everlasting.

He came up like a cork and back to the river-bank,
Put on his clothes in reverse order,
Returned to the house.

He suffered the enormous agonies of passion
Writing poems from the end backwards,
Brushing away tears that had not yet fallen.

Loving her wildly as the day regressed towards morning
He watched her swinging in the garden, growing younger,
Bare-foot, straw-hatted.

And when she was gone and the house and the swing and
                                                daylight
There was an instant's pause before it began all over,
The reel unrolling towards the river.

From *Daily Living*

Visiting

The stick, the fan, the basket, the morning paper,
But first the task—hymn-books to be gathered
After the morning service. There's an old girl playing

'Jealousy' from sheet-music at the piano,
('I make my fingers work. It's the arthritis.')
I walk with my mother outside round the garden.

Some rage simmers in all of us all the time.
I know her rage as mine. 'Oh, these
Old women—' she says, as though a mutinous girl,

Who all her life has so compliantly
Deferred to accident, event, and time.
Something behind the drained blue of her eyes

Flashes. We go inside and gather up
The basket, stick, and fan, and the unread
News of another world. We say good-bye.

Daily I leave so and am glad to go.
Daily she tells me of her troubled dreams.
I listen. Could not bear to tell her mine.

Who?

Who, then, was 'Auntie Molly'? No one now
Can tell me who she was: or how it was
She and my Mother shared a rented house
One summer for a fortnight—we took a train
And from the station trudged a country road.
I know she worked year-long and lived alone
Somewhere with a strange name, like Rooty Hill.

Postoffice-Store-in-one sold bread and milk.
Returning to our house we scuffed along
Cloth-hatted, sandalled, kicking at the stones.
Mother and Auntie Molly walked ahead
And suddenly Mother stopped, threw back her head
And laughed and laughed there in the dusty road.
We were amazed to hear our Mother laugh.

The fowl-yard fence sagged with ripe passion-fruit,
We bought cream in a jug. At night we sat
Around the lamp-lit table, colouring in.
In bed, near sleep, we'd hear the rise and fall
Of their grave voices—hers, and Auntie Molly's,
Whom no one now would know; who made my Mother
Laugh joyfully in the middle of the road.

Oodgeroo of the tribe Noonuccal (formerly Kath Walker)

Daisy Bindi

Slavery at Roy Hill, to our shame profound,
Wages for the blacks nil all the year round,
Slavers given free hand by police consent,
Winked at obligingly by Government.
But a woman warrior where aid there was none
Led her dark people till the fight was won.

Salute to a spirit fine,
Daisy of Nullagine,
Who unaided resolutely
Dared to challenge slavery.

Tall Daisy Bindi, she rode like a man,
Mustering and stockwork from when dawn began,
And long chores indoors that made life bleak
Year after weary year for nothing a week,
Till Daisy of the stout heart organized her clan
To strike for native justice and the plain rights of man.

High praise and honour to
Daisy of the noongahs who
Fought and routed tyranny,
Dared to challenge slavery.

Oh, the boss men threatened and the boss men swore,
They called the police in to help break the law,
And dark men and women were forced and assailed,
For fighting degradation they were bashed and jailed,
But Daisy the militant no man subdued,
Who championed her people out of servitude.

Gifts

'I will bring you love,' said the young lover,
'A glad light to dance in your dark eye.
Pendants I will bring of the white bone,
And gay parrot feathers to deck your hair.'

But she only shook her head.

'I will put a child in your arms,' he said,
'Will be a great headman, great rain-maker.
I will make remembered songs about you
That all the tribes in all the wandering camps
Will sing for ever.'

But she was not impressed.

'I will bring you the still moonlight on the lagoon,
And steal for you the singing of all the birds;
I will bring down the stars of heaven to you,
And put the bright rainbow into your hand.'

'No,' she said, 'bring me tree-grubs.'

Dawn Wail for the Dead

Dim light of daybreak now
Faintly over the sleeping camp.
Old lubra first to wake remembers:
First thing every dawn
Remember the dead, cry for them.
Softly at first her wail begins,
One by one as they wake and hear
Join in the cry, and the whole camp
Wails for the dead, the poor dead
Gone from here to the Dark Place:
They are remembered.
Then it is over, life now,
Fires lit, laughter now,
And a new day calling.

Last of His Tribe

Change is the law. The new must oust the old.
I look at you and am back in the long ago,
Old pinnaroo lonely and lost here,
Last of your clan.
Left only with your memories, you sit
And think of the gay throng, the happy people,
The voices and the laughter
All gone, all gone,
And you remain alone.

I asked and you let me hear
The soft vowelly tongue to be heard now
No more for ever. For me
You enact old scenes, old ways, you who have used
Boomerang and spear.
You singer of ancient tribal songs,
You leader once in the corroboree,
You twice in fierce tribal fights
With wild enemy blacks from over the river,
All gone, all gone. And I feel
The sudden sting of tears, Willie Mackenzie
In the Salvation Army Home.
Displaced person in your own country,
Lonely in teeming city crowds,
Last of your tribe.

No More Boomerang

No more boomerang
No more spear;
Now all civilized—
Colour bar and beer.

No more corroboree,
Gay dance and din.
Now we got movies,
And pay to go in.

No more sharing
What the hunter brings.
Now we work for money,
Then pay it back for things.

Now we track bosses
To catch a few bob,
Now we go walkabout
On bus to the job.

One time naked,
Who never knew shame;
Now we put clothes on
To hide whatsaname.

No more gunya,
Now bungalow,
Paid by hire purchase
In twenty year or so.

Lay down the stone axe,
Take up the steel,
And work like a nigger
For a white man meal.

No more firesticks
That made the whites scoff.
Now all electric,
And no better off.

Bunyip he finish
Now got instead
White fella Bunyip,
Call him Red.

Abstract picture now—
What they coming at?
Cripes, in our caves we
Did better than that.

Black hunted wallaby,
White hunt dollar;
White fella witch-doctor
Wear dog-collar.

No more message-stick;
Lubras and lads
Got television now,
Mostly ads.

Lay down the woomera,
Lay down the waddy.
Now we got atom-bomb,
End *every*body.

Gwen Harwood

Ebb-Tide

Now that you have no word for me
I bring your bitter silence here
where the sea rustles from the land
seaward, its whispered meaning clear.

My young son chases, stone in hand,
a sandcrabs' rattling greyblue army.

He stones the scuttling host, and gathers
one crippled prize. Cannot decide
which is its head. As dying claws
tickle his palm, he laughs. The tide
withdraws for his delight. We pause
at every pool. The mind surrenders

its agony to littoral creatures
rocked in the comfort of the shore's
unvarying seasons. A smooth spine
held in my idle fingers scores
a name in sand as the gulls sign
the windless water with your features.

I have one picture of you taken
picnicking somewhere: mountains, clouds
beyond a pier; incredibly blue
water surrounds you, masts and shrouds
pattern unheard-of azure. You
smile there for ever. Time has shaken

life from the sea, flung on dry land
bones that got upright, fleshed their wild
sea-creature grins, and learned the weight
of earth. I run beside my child
stoning the crabs with mindless hate.
The sea withdraws from the gold sand.

Carnal Knowledge I

Roll back, you fabulous animal
be human, sleep. I'll call you up
from water's dazzle, wheat-blond hills,
clear light and open-hearted roses,
this day's extravagance of blue
stored like a pulsebeat in the skull.

Content to be your love, your fool,
your creature tender and obscene
I'll bite sleep's innocence away
and wake the flesh my fingers cup
to build a world from what's to hand,
new energies of light and space

wings for blue distance, fins to sweep
the obscure caverns of your heart,
a tongue to lift your sweetness close
leaf-speech against the window-glass
a memory of chaos weeping
mute forces hammering for shape

sea-strip and sky-strip held apart
for earth to form its hills and roses
its landscape from our blind caresses,
blue air, horizon, water-flow,
bone to my bone I grasp the world.
But what you are I do not know.

Carnal Knowledge II

Grasshoppers click and whirr.
Stones grow in the field.
Autumnal warmth is sealed
in a gold skin of light
on darkness plunging down
to earth's black molten core.

Earth has no more to yield.
Her blond grasses are dry.
   Nestling my cheek against
   the hollow of your thigh
   I lay cockeyed with love
   in the most literal sense.

Your eyes, kingfisher blue.
This was the season, this
the light, the halcyon air.
Our window framed this place.
If there were music here,
insectile, abstract, bare,

it would bless no human ear.
Shadows lie with the stones.
Bury our hearts, perhaps
they'll strike it rich in earth's
black marrow, crack, take root,
bring forth vines, blossom, fruit.

Roses knocked on the glass.
Wine like a running stream
no evil spell could cross
flowed round the house of touch.
God grant me drunkenness
if this is sober knowledge,

song to melt sea and sky
apart, and lift these hills
from the shadow of what was,
and roll them back, and lie
in naked ignorance
in the hollow of your thigh.

Father and Child

I   Barn Owl

Daybreak: the household slept.
I rose, blessed by the sun.
A horny fiend, I crept
out with my father's gun.
Let him dream of a child
obedient, angel-mild—

old No-Sayer, robbed of power
by sleep. I knew my prize
who swooped home at this hour
with daylight-riddled eyes
to his place on a high beam
in our old stables, to dream

light's useless time away.
I stood, holding my breath,
in urine-scented hay,
master of life and death,
a wisp-haired judge whose law
would punish beak and claw.

My first shot struck. He swayed,
ruined, beating his only
wing, as I watched, afraid
by the fallen gun, a lonely
child who believed death clean
and final, not this obscene

bundle of stuff that dropped,
and dribbled through loose straw
tangling in bowels, and hopped
blindly closer. I saw
those eyes that did not see
mirror my cruelty

while the wrecked thing that could
not bear the light nor hide
hobbled in its own blood.
My father reached my side,
gave me the fallen gun.
'End what you have begun.'

I fired. The blank eyes shone
once into mine, and slept.
I leaned my head upon
my father's arm, and wept,
owl-blind in early sun
for what I had begun.

II *Nightfall*

Forty years, lived or dreamed:
what memories pack them home.
Now the season that seemed
incredible is come.
Father and child, we stand
in time's long-promised land.

Since there's no more to taste
ripeness is plainly all.
Father, we pick our last
fruits of the temporal.
Eighty years old, you take
this late walk for my sake.

Who can be what you were?
Link your dry hand in mine,
my stick-thin comforter.
Far distant suburbs shine
with great simplicities.
Birds crowd in flowering trees,

sunset exalts its known
symbols of transience.
Your passionate face is grown
to ancient innocence.
Let us walk for this hour
as if death had no power

or were no more than sleep.
Things truly named can never
vanish from earth. You keep
a child's delight for ever
in birds, flowers, shivery-grass—
I name them as we pass.

'*Be your tears wet?*' You speak
as if air touched a string
near breaking-point. Your cheek
brushes on mine. Old king,
your marvellous journey's done.
Your night and day are one

as you find with your white stick
the path on which you turn
home with the child once quick
to mischief, grown to learn
what sorrows, in the end,
no words, no tears can mend.

Return of the Native

The big house is turned into flats, the last camphor laurel
cut down, alas; the street paved, the cool weatherboard suburb
gone trendy with fancy brick; but new roses spill
their old abundance of scent, and across the kerb

as if this were a film, a Mintie wrapper blows.
So cut to two freckled children unwrapping Minties
in their camphor laurel house, and from wide windows
let the sounds of teacups and voices and laughter rise.

It is late afternoon, and the towering cumulus gather
over city, suburb and treehouse as everyone tells
silly stories. A pause. A rich baritone voice is clear:
'Well, a gentleman knows where he is if the police own the
    brothels.'

The grown-ups shriek, and repeat the curious line.
Heaven cracks open. The children run, drenched, inside,
and the girl, who learns like a parrot, repeats it again
and is slapped into tears without knowing how she has offended.

And Freddy, who said it while managing his tea
with his hand and his hook says, 'She didn't understand,'
and talks about Little Pitchers and says he's sorry.
(He told me once: 'When the Germans shot off my hand

'God gave me this hook, it's much better for carrying parcels.'
I believed the curving steel grew out of his arm.)
But it's time for some good old songs, and music quells
the world's injustice, and clears away the storm.

My taxi is waiting. The driver puts down his book.
It's Volume Two of the brick-red paperback Popper.
I say, 'Full Marx?' He grins, 'Half. Have you had a good look?
Was that your old home? Do you like what they've done to her?

'Do you like what they've done to this old State of yours?
I'm a useless M.A. It's no use whingeing, but.
You can't sing hymns in the park, and the police own the
    parlours.
But I've a sick wife and a kid, so I keep my mouth shut.

'Ban Uranium, one bald tyre, they'll have you off.
If you're sporting a Jesus Saves they'll let you go
without tyres or lights. You'd better go back down south.'
I remember Freddy singing 'My old Shako',

and would like to say, he'd given a hand for freedom
and would use his hook if anyone threatened his rights.
But the truth is, he'd have voted to build the Bomb
and to clean the long-haired larrikins out of the streets.

Turn like a jewel that small clear scene in your head:
cloud-blaze, leaf-glitter, loved faces, a radiant voice
singing 'Fifty years ago . . .' Though you summon the dead
you cannot come as a child to your father's house.

Mother Who Gave Me Life

Mother who gave me life
I think of women bearing
women. Forgive me the wisdom
I would not learn from you.

It is not for my children I walk
on earth in the light of the living.
It is for you, for the wild
daughters becoming women,

anguish of seasons burning
backward in time to those other
bodies, your mother, and hers
and beyond, speech growing stranger

on thresholds of ice, rock, fire,
bones changing, head inclining
to monkey bosom, lemur breast,
guileless milk of the word.

I prayed you would live to see
Halley's Comet a second time.
The Sister said, When she died
she was folding a little towel.

You left the world so, having lived
nearly thirty thousand days:
a fabric of marvels folded
down to a little space.

At our last meeting I closed
the ward door of heavy glass
between us, and saw your face
crumple, fine threadbare linen

worn, still good to the last,
then, somehow, smooth to a smile
so I should not see your tears.
Anguish: remembered hours:

a lamp on embroidered linen,
my supper set out, your voice
calling me in as darkness
falls on my father's house.

Bone Scan

Thou hast searched me and known me. Thou knowest my
downsitting and mine uprising.

Psalm 139

In the twinkling of an eye,
in a moment, all is changed:
on a small radiant screen
(honeydew melon green)
are my scintillating bones.
Still in my flesh I see
the God who goes with me
glowing with radioactive
isotopes. This is what he
at last allows a mortal
eye to behold: the grand
supporting frame complete
(but for the wisdom teeth),
the friend who lives beneath
appearances, alive
with light. Each glittering bone
assures me: you are known.

Nan McDonald

The Lonely Fire

Silent under the moon the white shore road
Unwinds its miles. No leaping fish has stirred
The wide still water, clear and dark close in
And farther out a sheet of milky silver
The great black hills of bush ring all around.
From the leaves of beaten metal no cry of a bird,
From the naked gleaming bough of the gum, from the pools
Of inky shade, no sound.

And now in the township under the rocky height
No one's awake and abroad. Not even a cat
Hunts moths and bright-eyed mice in the long pale grass.
In the huddled houses only the moon's chilled white
Glitters back from the small blind panes. No open door,
No warmth of voice or light.

Only red on the wharf one fire burns,
Only the madman's voice makes broken song;
His hollow, bearded face haunts the smoke, returns
And fades like the veering of his derelict mind
That now by no day or night, by shout or flame,
Can signal to its kind.

How far has he walked since he sang in the orange orchards—
Golden fruit and glossy leaves in the winter sun—
Till the picking was over and the men paid off,
How many miles of white road since that sun went down?
And cold and hunger crept out of the dusk to his side,
Fear crouched in the shadowy bush—but all that's done.
He'll travel no farther—how far from the young man's grace,
His pride, his hope, to this place?

O you behind your blank windows, lift your heads, listen!
You cannot shut out his voice, for it is your own
And mine, and Man's—lost, mad enough for scorning;
We have come down our roads to this ending, each alone,
And now must walk with ghosts in the silver night
And fear the bloodstained morning.

No answer. It may be you are wiser than I:
Something strange, enormous, is abroad tonight.
Let me find my hole, too, burrowing in blankets for fear
Of this white hush of water, earth, and sky.
Is it the death of the world already beginning?
Or is it that in the stillness God leans near
To hear the madman's cry?

The Mountain Road: Crete, 1941

(For Bill)

The roads of all your life closed in that night
To the one road through the mountains to the sea;
And that one night was all your travelling time
Lest by the brutal daybreak you should be
Trapped on the narrow ledge for sacrifice
And all your bitter striving thrown away;
And as the steep miles and black hours wore on,
Around the next bend, straining hope would say,
The rocks must part, the way must turn downhill—
But ever the dark road wound upward still.

You had come a long march since you watched the sun
Crawl slow and murderous down a glare of sky,
While the swooping terror that had hunted you
Across the open ground shot screaming by,
Spattered your covering leaves to deathly foam,
Seeking you all those loud mad hours of light;
And dusk had fallen like the shade of God,
But thickened soon to this hot, moonless night;
And the dark's desperate need was swift to kill
Its fragile peace—and the way toiled upward still.

Beyond that black wall lay the brave grey ships
And the vast shining freedom of the sea—
The sea that breaks on endless alien coasts
With the old, loved voice of childhood memory;
So that its tides rise in the heart like tears
And but to wind it on the freshening gale
Is to come home, be done with wars and wounds—
But all this seemed some far-off fairytale.
Men so betrayed trust only what is ill
And that the road for ever winds uphill.

Nor any more remembering that stream,
Snow-cold beyond the blazing village, brought
Its blissful chill to seared throats, sweated skins,
All that returned was the flames' fury caught
In eyes dried with long waking, so their stare
Smeared on the eastward mirk its red and made
An angry dawn yet earlier than its hour—
At best, too early—and the heart, dismayed,
Had cried defeat but for the flogging will
As the road swung, and turned once more uphill.

And all along men fell and slept, more lost,
More piteous as they drew their shallow breath,
Than the still dead, who would not wake too late
To see the bright sky scarred with shrieking death.
But in the end all these things dropped away
As one huge labour gripped the darkening brain—
How each dull, weighted boot must be moved on,
The swaying body thrust—and yet in pain
At every turn the unwanted hope surged still,
And the sick ebb, and the road once more uphill.

This was a tale once wildly strange to me—
That you should go such ways, and I not there—
But I have come to know that deadly road,
The windings of that black snake of despair;
And you around the last turn met the sky,
The sudden, sweet drop downward to the shore,
And, feeling the deck lift to the long swell,
You smiled, and fell asleep, and feared no more;
But I in the dark pass, with heart struck chill,
See the east pale—and the way goes upward still.

Sleep

In shallows of sleep I lingered then to see
Again the beauties and blessings of the day
As one looks back, the white surf at his knee
To hillsides rich with leaves, soaring away
From yellow sand to morning sky, the blue
Heaven-well too deep for memory to possess,
Till snow-rush foam and glass-green swell must woo
His heart from land joy to sea happiness.

But headlong now down rocky heights to sleep
I run, as convicts ran, not looking back
To lash, chain, and black cell, hearing the deep
Call through the blood-bay of the following pack,
Over the cliff-edge hurtle, down and down,
And, thanking God for His dark mercies, drown.

The Hawk

I came out in the morning
And he was there—
The pale hawk, alone
On the lightning-blasted tree.
The fierce and burning air
Struck at my lifted face—
I had not thought to see him
Again in this place.

Ash-grey on the grey wood,
White on the hot white sky,
A ghost he seemed, from the years
When the deep forest stood
Around that one stark tree
(A child, I saw them die
Felled as the city spread),
But he turned, and down his long
Curved wing the shadow darkened,
Showed him alive and strong.

He turned his flat, cruel head
And looked out on the land,
The baking roofs of the suburb,
The dusty streets, and beyond,
The paddocks bleached with drought,
The shimmering glare of sand
In the dry bed of the creek,
The dreadful blackened miles,
The twisted iron and rubble
Where there were towns last week.

He did not open his beak,
He made no cry,
But I looked in his savage eye,
I heard him speak.
'You thought the hawk had fled
And dared no more come near?
That you had driven me out
As you drove beyond your city
The famine, the fear?
It has been a long time,' he said,
'But I am here.'

Daisy Utemorrah

Our Mother Land

Our dream and our past is buried under the ground.
When the sun rises and begins another day
all is empty, ground and hill shake on us,
overwhelmed with people everywhere.
The dream the past—where does it stand now?

The burun burun whirrs in the night time
And the owl calling!
And the dingo howling!
The moon shines on the water, all is ended—
and the dreamtime gone.

Black Man

I am thinking of the mountains,
memories tumbling out of my head
Now all is gone.
What must I do?
Good times and bad I spend in civilization.
Will I go back to my hills and mountains
and hear the whistle of the curlews all night long,
echoes of the rushing stream,
the wind rustling by and the owls calling.
The frog croaks and sleeps,
I long to see the stars smile down
at me!

Nancy Keesing

Cicada Song

This leafy day of drunken summer
Greengrocer and Orange Drummer,
Yellow Monday and Cherry Nose,
The moment that the sun rose
To make the air more hot than heat
To burn our ears, your beat, drum, beat
Began. And now the evening's here
You, drunkards, stagger down the air
In long glissades from branch to ground
With spurts of agitated sound,
Until in dark and noisy night
A Black Prince plummets to the light,
Comes whirring through the kitchen door,
Skitters across the polished floor,

And on my hand is drumming long
Like any sot who loves his song . . . .
        Might then the true word set him free
From some strange, heat-dazed sorcery?
And Margery, you child of fable,
See, standing by this very table
A prince indeed?
                    We'll end his spree
In the safe liquidambar tree—
Some things are better left unknown
Lest, once the exorcism's shown,
Not only Prince, but Cherry Nose or
Floury Baker and Greengrocer
Come clamouring; and who would wish
A Yellow Monday in the flesh? . . .

Then let us leave this tipsy air
and cool in sober sleep, my dear.

Detective Story

Only the corpse on the floor was out of it all,
The sprawled insensate hulk with timeless eyes
That would never see his mad old aunt again.
—Wringing her hands in the corner; chirping cries
Like those of unfledged nestlings flopped from her lips:
His mad old aunt weeping against the wall.

Nor could he see the girl, the bitter blonde
Slumped in the armchair and regarding him;
She'd bought the dagger, she of your first guess,
And he cannot tell the truth, being over the rim,
Buried the second day, gone from the story.
Far past the edge of the shadow, there beyond

The family circle, solid, immutable,
His box of tricks neat, ready for the fray
The Man from the Yard stands smiling.
It was luck that caught him here on holiday
In a lost village of one dumb constable
Sullenly puzzled by the inscrutable.

Here we leave something to your imagination—
The scratch on the window, fat butler's evidence,
The lines from Hamlet; a well-hidden clue
Pushed through the ivy on the backyard fence;
Quaint flutterings of the aunt about the house
And village comments on the great sensation.

His aunt it was, of course, for an addled reason.
She who recalled him as a grubby boy
And often scrubbed him raw at a day's end;
She who chose well a favourite game or toy
Could not accept man's toys not of her choosing.
She thought, this way, to keep him for a season.

Craftily planned and had him for a visit,
His life to prove her art and loving care:
Then, perfect attainment, no further aim or striving—
The shattering bleakness of profound despair
With nothing proved, an ear-to-a-mistress nothing.
You could read the book, but it isn't important, is it?

This daft old dame, lonely, puzzled and mild,
Within her withered arms held only dreams,
Fancies, dissected throughout two hundred pages
While police tramp in and out and torchlight gleams
Not the first crone to pin a dream on a knife
Nor yet the first who'd kill to keep her child.

Dorothy Hewett

In Moncur Street

It's twenty years ago and more
since first I came to Moncur Street,
and lived with Aime and Alf among
the boarders on the second floor.

The stew was burnt, the budgie sang,
as Aime walked home the church-bells rang,
she banged the pots, ring-ding-a-ding,
she'd lost at Housie in the Spring.

But Sammy Smiles (that lovely man),
still visits her on Saturday,
Beat runs a book, and little Fay
whines in the stairwell every day
        in Moncur Street
        in Moncur Street.

Alf rose before the morning light,
and took a chopper in his hand;
he chopped and chopped in Oxford Street.
'Alf runs around without his head,
he's like a chook,' said Aime
        and sighed
for Sammy Smiles (that lovely man),

And Sunny Corner where she played
at 'Ladies' in the willow's shade.
At sunset by the empty shops
they swapped their dusty acid drops:
who lounges in the crystal air,
but Sammy Smiles, with marcelled hair!

I woke up in the darkest night,
knew all the world had caught alight.
The surf was pounding in the weather,
and Moncur Street was mine forever.
The little bat upon the stair
came out and flapped: it wasn't there,
the snapshot album turned and turned,
the stew caught fire, the budgie burned,
the pensioners at drafts and dreams,
picked bugs between their trouser seams.

And Sammy Smiles (that lovely man!)
and Aime and Alf and little Fay,
and Beat and Bert and betting slips,
the man I loved, the child I bore,
have all gone under Bondi's hills,
and will return here nevermore,
        in Moncur Street
        in Moncur Street.

Alf starts up his steady snore,
'Them Bondi sandhill's paved with gold,
I could've bought them for a song.'

The home brew bursts behind the door.
Aime lies upon her back and sighs:
'In Sunny Corner by the store
Sam kissed me once when I turned four.'

Dreams are deep and love is long:
she turns upon her other side.

Miss Hewett's Shenanigans

They call, 'The Prince has come',
& I swan down in astrakan & fur,
the lemon curtains blown against the light,
the scent of lilac on the balconies.
In the entrance hall
the Prince is standing
                staring at my thighs.
He mounts, how cold the marble
underneath my buttocks.
As he rides he calls me
                'whore' & 'princess'.
A platinum crooner, old as Alice Faye,
belts out bad ragtime in the empty ballroom.
The Prince, buttoning his fly,
is doing push-ups & demanding saunas.
Two giant Ghanians smile & kiss my hand.

Snow piles like roses
                up against the panes,
the waiter brings 'Ogonyok',
SINYAVSKY'S FLED & SOLZHENITSYN'S EXILED.
The lights all fail,
the electrician's pinching bulbs
from the chandeliers, shoving them
                down his shirtfront.
Outside in the dark at Lenin's tomb
they endlessly queue for weeping
                at the waxworks.

The Prince is in the Conference Hall,
listening through headphones
to a speech in seven languages.
Handsome Yugoslav colonels
discreetly try my doorknobs.

Exhausted, we sleep among carved bears
with ashtrays in their paws,
he refuses, once again, to consummate our marriage.

Next day we catch the Trans-Siberian
to Peking; from the observation car
we watch two wolves pacing out the train,
the Prince throws pennies to Manchurian children.
On the Great Wall he lets the wind blow
through my hair, in the Forbidden City
we listen to the clockwork nightingale.

By Aeroflot we fly in to Berlin,
the Prince will not declare his Camels
            at Checkpoint Charlie,
(An international incident is narrowly averted.)
In the country house of Hitler's wormy mistress
we row on a lake circled with tuber roses.
The Prince, a playboy in a boater hat,
is picking the plastic flowers
            off Heine's statue;
denouncing Nazis he pisses in the Weimar fountain,
rides with a chignoned spy
            down Karl Marx Allee.
Tiring of this,
        we climb across the Wall,
the Vopos bow, goosestep & fire a round,
the bullets spurt,
we show our elegant heels.
In West Berlin the Prince
calls for his breakfast, on TV
Brezhnev has cancer, enters the Mayo clinic.

The Prince leafs through his autographs,
Picasso, Gandhi, Garbo, Pasternak,
calls Nabokov long distance, mounts me,
yawns, the Brandenburg Gate whirls
& explodes in the pale autumn air.
Next morning he leaves,
            taking all my roubles.

Suffering from migraine
I enter a Retreat
among the Alps I write him
endless letters.

The corridors are full of parasites,
consumptives haemorrhage in their sleety deckchairs,
in the white nights I masturbate my pillows.

  An aerogramme arrives,
  'The Prince is dead!'
I take up seances,
each night we couple,
circling the empty ballroom
     to 'Moscow Nights'.
Cockroaches rustle, my thrombosed knee
reeks of its vodka bandage,
the dust settles from the chandelier
    on his bald head . . .

Madame Bovary

In the village ghetto hand to mouth
the funereal carriage spokes
flash by the park the bridge across
the harbour smiling in the courtyard
on the balcony smiling the camera clicks
the mirrored cadenced voices
faking it Bovary the sentimental arsenic
lady is she the one you met the one
you knew so well?

the rose bowls full of early summer's petals
on glass tabletops she leaves love-letters
the drapes looped back the autumn light
falls in great shafts through the floorlength windows
outside under the birch trees a girl abandoned
her black cloak scuffs the leaves
obliterating everything . . .

the garden's empty in the last light
between the avenues twin horses plunge
the carriage rocks without a driver
running through bare trees the whipbirds in
the topmost branches torment her
back to childhood where a room waits by a river
waterfalled in light . . .

flee from this garden in the house of sighs
love rocks the bed she shared with many lovers
a note left on a pillow barefoot through golden gorse
she drives with one dark man & then another
the husband waits   the children cry   alone
she takes the powder   her back arches in parody
the grey brothers stand at her right shoulder
the one you meet   the one you knew so well
Bovary   the sentimental arsenic lady.

Anniversary

Death is in the air—

today is the anniversary of his death in October
(he would have been thirty-one)
I went home to High Street
& couldn't feed the new baby
my milk had dried up
so I sat holding him numbly
looking for the soft spot on the top of his head
while they fed me three more librium
you're only crying for yourself he said
but I kept on saying *It's the waste I can't bear.*

All that winter we lived
in the longest street in the world
he used to walk to work in the dark
on the opposite side of the street
somebody always walked with him but they never met
he could only hear the boots
& when he stopped they stopped.

The new baby swayed in a canvas cot lacing his fingers
I worried in case he got curvature of the spine
Truby King said a baby needed firm support
he was a very big bright baby
the cleaner at the Queen Vic said every morning
you mark my words that kid's been here before.

The house was bare & cold with a false gable
we had no furniture only a double mattress
on the floor a big table & two deal chairs
each morning I dressed the baby in a shrunken jacket

& caught the bus home to my mother's to nurse the child
who was dying   the house had bay windows
hidden under fir trees smothered in yellow roses
the child sat dwarfed at the end of the polished table
pale as death in the light of his four candles
singing *Little Boy Blue.*

I pushed the pram to the telephone box
I'm losing my milk I told her   *I want to bring him
home to die*   *Home* she said   *you left
home a long time ago to go with that man.*

I pushed them both through the park
over the dropped leaves (his legs were crippled)
a magpie swooped down black out of the sky
& pecked his forehead   a drop of blood splashed on
his wrist   he started to cry

It took five months & everybody was angry
because the new baby was alive & cried for attention
pollen sprinkled his cheeks under the yellow roses.

When he died it was like everybody else
in the public ward with the screens around him
the big bruises spreading on his skin
his hand came up out of the sheets *don't cry*
he said   *don't be sad*
I sat there overweight in my Woolworth's dress
not telling anybody in case they kept him alive
with another transfusion—

        Afterwards I sat by the gas fire
in my old dressing-gown turning over the photographs
wondering why I'd drunk all that stout
& massaged my breasts every morning to be
        a good mother.

For The Glory of God & of Gwendoline

O Gwen so long the mute the burning Sappho
Lancelot's lady & King Arthur's consort
invite me in for we can have such sport
dissecting skirmishes   the battles fought
over the topless towers of this court

where Merlin rages & the moonlight falls
to fill the dangling armour on the walls:
Art is the great enchanter   let us go.

The young   the wild   the foolish & the brave
rave round the frontiers or cross at night,
they'll have to let us in without a fight,
we are the ladies fashioned for delight;
O we will be well met by moonlight Gwen
at that round table with King Arthur's men:
this Camelot has fallen on evil days

it needs our presence to improve the tone,
we'll bring our manuscripts they can't refuse
a little criticism helps the Muse,
maybe it's not too late to bring the news
that you & I intend to light a fuse
in Camelot . . . . O Gwen
we've always had a nice way with the men
& this time we won't operate alone:

we'll keep our beds we wont rage up & down
we've learnt a lot from living long outside
their wars & wonderments yet we can ride
with Lancelot & Merlin side by side,
you've changed a bit since you were Arthur's bride;
we two, outstripping all the dazzling men,
will keep their swords for bodkins lovely Gwen,
O Gwendoline   we'll scandalize this town:

and do not ask me Gwen where are the snows
of yesteryear . . . the way to Camelot
once known it can never be forgot,
the horses steam & all the knights are hot,
a good hard ride & we'll outstrip the lot,
our problem is   the company of men
has always been a pleasure to us Gwen,
maybe the Grail is not for us, who knows

who'll see the Grail, who is it that will choose
to fuck & fast & masturbate & pray
with inky fingers till his hair turns grey,
because we're weaker vessels must we stay
within four walls as if its holy day
& live a life of discipline & order?
Merlin has told me it's across the border,
I say let's ride we've nothing left to lose.

Owl

Driving all day
through the tingle forest
in a splatter of rain
at night
we turned off the highway
the white track
sloped towards a sky
scudded with cloud
a giant owl
flapped in our faces
covering the windscreen
with feathers
it sat in the headlights
dazzled
staring us down

for a long time
it stayed there
the boughs overreaching
the silence outside
then spreading its wings
it flew
under cover of darkness.

Later I saw him
lurching down
the one bleak street
of the town
the feathered legs
hidden in jeans
the fingers lopped off
to a claw
in the local sawmill
beak blue with cold
one eye blazing
under a limp felt hat.

Grace Perry

The page will not contain you

The page will not contain you
I cannot make a man from an ink blot
perception is illusion
reality is not cockled in the dream
my work can never be my life
not for a minute
vision is sharper than truth
and twice as final
we delude ourselves to talk of love
there is no chain between the separate bodies
we link ourselves together
with silk scarves inscribed 'forever'
I cannot write your name

I am object beyond all expression
daily I chisel my cemetery of words
I do not wake the dead to rise again.

Leaving the House

What if the walls collapsed like playing cards
                     mahogany
                       enamel panels
and the wind whisked them away?
The black birdsleg supports
were not designed to hold up centuries.
Eaves licked skytongue blue
could be devoured entirely
and windows that have confronted
water so many years
slide down the dune
                   one high tide
slip under the froth
regroup upon the calm far out.
It would not be difficult for the fence to fall;
it leans already.
Both sides grass stretches, grows impatient.
I am afraid each time I go away

climbing the road out of the valley
afraid to look back from the cliffbend.
Perhaps by next time it will have happened
as if we had never been
the land restored — a sandhill between pine trees
banksia skeletons   hibiscus   oleander
knotted irrevocably as lovers on the west slope
and to the east the fringe of marram grass
the sand curving under the sea.

I am afraid each time I nudge the last hill
turn the high corner —
there is no doubt.
The car rolls down black road
sunlight fires the faces of all the windows
the eaves are on straight
the roof precise
any defects are less obvious up close
I was sure the paint was peeling
the stain was dry.
The road ends here —
like love
arrival is a little miracle —
once more the walls accept me.
I am home.

Glen Tomasetti

Don't Be Too Polite, Girls!

1

We're really on the way, girls, really on the way!
Hooray for equal pay, girls, hooray for equal pay!
They'll give it to ten percent of us in spite of all their fears,
But do they really need to make us wait three years?
Though equal pay in principle is now a woman's right,
To turn it into practice, we must show a little fight,
We fear male disapproval, if to argue we decide,
The boss fears for his bank account, the husband for his pride.

Chorus
Don't be too polite, girls, don't be too polite!
Show a little fight, girls, show a little fight!
Don't be fearful of offending in case you get the sack,
Just recognise your value and we won't look back.

2

I work as a waitress. My working mates are men,
Do I have to go to court to prove I work as hard as them?
The diner knows the food, the bill, the tips are just the same,
Well, tell me why my pay is less and how am I to blame?
I sew up shirts and trousers in the clothing trade,
Since men don't do the job I can't ask to be better paid.
The people at the top have rarely offered something more
Until the people underneath were walking out the door.

CHORUS

3

They say a man needs more to keep his children and his wife,
What are the needs of a woman who leads a double working life?
When the whistle blows for knock-off, it's not her time for fun,
She goes home to start the job that's not yet paid and never done.
The employer needs his profit, but the argument is weak,
Compared with how a woman needs eight dollars more a week,
Eight dollars more of butter and eggs and fruit and bread and meat
And a bit aside to buy some shoes for all the growing feet.

CHORUS

4

'We can't afford to pay you', say the masters in their wrath,
But woman says, 'Just cut the coat according to the cloth!
If the economy won't stand it, here's the answer, boys,
Cut out the wild extravagance on the new war toys!'
All among the bull, girls, all among the bull,
Keep your hearts full, girls, keep your hearts full!
What good is a man as a doormat, or following at heel?
It's not their pants we're after, it's a fair square deal.

CHORUS

Fay Zwicky

Isaac Babel's Fiddle Reaches the Indian Ocean

*Mr Zagursky ran a factory of infant prodigies, a factory of Jewish
dwarfs in lace collars and patent-leather pumps. He hunted them out
in the slums of Moldavanka, in the evil-smelling courtyards of the
Old Market . . . My father decided that I should emulate them . . .
I was fettered to the instruments of my torture, and dragged them
about with me . . . One day I left home laden like a beast of burden
with violin-case, violin music, and twelve roubles in cash—payment
for a month's tuition. I was going along Nezhin Street; to get to
Zagursky's I should have turned into Dvoryanskaya but instead of
that I . . . found myself at the harbour . . . So began my liberation.*
                                              Isaac Babel, *Awakening*

Just try and cast a piano
In the sea
Romantically.
Take it from me, you'll
Never make it.

I tried it once
Or twice. My
Polished albatross
Kicked me as we
Sank through
Coral gardens.

And rose, rosewood
Bird and I,
Buoyed by
Bubbling spirals past
The emerald gills,
The darting purple fins,

Up through the silent
Gardens beckoning
In dappled solar tracks
To break the
Limpid bounds of an
Elysium aquamarine.

What happened when you left
That day? A day of frozen
Lakes and weighted birches,
Fleeing mittenless
The fond solicitude
That sealed your case

And thrust you talentless
Upon Zagursky's stoop to
Sit among the drooping
Ugly boys, your eyes
Intent upon their
Bruised necks, their neat

Doll's feet; Anchises' tadpoles
In withered velvet suits
Bearing their father, *theotokoi*,
Upon their bows to
101st street, East, the
Summerhearted phoenix land.

You'd seen your father
Touch his cap and bow
While Cossacks tore
His store apart.
Meanwhile your heart
Quickened with Dumas,

Stopped with Turgenev
(Disguised by Sevčik
On the stand). It was your
Judashand that flung the
Fiddle, spent the rouble
For Zagursky's care into

Odessa's sandbar—whose voice
Did you obey that day you
Sounded out the waterfront?
Hydrophobic shoot of land-locked
Scholars, febrile storekeepers
And gaunt Iberian rabbis in their caves.

The milling port that
Catapulted Heifetz, Elman
From the Tsarevitch's sight

Kept you, boy and man apart,
Heir to a single
Season of the heart.

You had no need to join
A brutal company;
(The world's a cossack haunt
In any case — Turgenev
Might have told you *that*),
What did you prove,

Master of silence? That you
Could pass the test
Your father failed, autumnal friend?
The silent salty wastes
Await us. These will
Get us in the end — meantime

The tendrils of the sea
Most tenderly embrace the
Adamantine gloss,
Time's rivulets are filtered,
Harmless, through each curled eyelet,
Every key is stilled.

The final feathered clamp
And suck of blind anemones
Rock the ancestral fate to jar
A host of ghostly swimmers,
Measuring their buoyant gravity
Beyond Odessa's black sandbar.

Summer Pogrom

Spade-bearded Grandfather, squat Lenin
In the snows of Donna Buang.
Your bicycle a wiry crutch, nomadic homburg
Alien, black, correct. Beneath, the curt defiant
Filamented eye. Does it count the dead
Between the Cossack horses' legs in Kovno?

Those dead who sleep in me, me dry
In a garden veiled with myrtle and oleander,
Desert snows that powder memory's track
Scoured by burning winds from eastern rocks,
Flushing the lobes of mind,
Fat white dormant flowrets.

Aggressive under dappled shade, girl in a glove;
Collins street in autumn,
Mirage of clattering crowds: Why don't you speak English?
I don't understand, *I don't understand!*
Sei nicht so ein Dummerchen, nobody cares.
Not for you the upreared hooves of Nikolai,
Eat your icecream, Kleine, *may his soul rot,*
These are good days.

Flared candles; the gift of children; love,
Need fulfilled, a name it has to have—how else to feel?
A radiance in the garden, the Electrolux man chats,
Cosy spectre of the afternoon's decay.
My eye his eye, the snows of Kovno cover us.
Is that my son bloodied against Isaac the Baker's door?

The tepid river's edge, reeds creak, rats' nests fold and quiver,
My feet sink in sand; the children splash and call, sleek
Little satyrs diamond-eyed reined to summer's roundabout,
Hiding from me. Must I excavate you,
Agents of my death? Hushed snows are deep, the
Dead lie deep in me.

Chicken

Tucked snug behind
Proscenium arch a
Baby's stoned to death:
The watchers sit in trembling furs,
Slumped with relief.
Beyond belief!
Come, let's get out before
The peak hour traffic snarls
The bridge. I've got cold chicken
In the fridge for supper—at least
I think I have. Those kids *will*
Gorge themselves. Oh go on,

You can pass! The light's already
Amber, hurry up! I'm dying for a
Cup of tea. Don't talk like that
To me, of all people!
Let's not quarrel, things are
Going so well: Ian's done his maths
And Nigel's sure to top his year.
You've worked so hard with
Him . . . what's that? I
Had to keep her home. You
Know that stomach thing she gets.
She'll be all right tomorrow.
Well, the wings have had it but
The breast's still there. Or
Part of it. You must be starving!
Can't see why we push ourselves to
Plays like that although I feel
The writer has a point to make.
Some cake? Oh damn, I
Gave it to that child next door;
I'm sure her mother doesn't
Feed her properly. What's the
Matter? Aren't you feeling well?
It'll pass. There's Dexsal in the
Cupboard and a glass is
Right in front of you.
All right, I'll come up later—
What a mess they leave the
Place! Did you say she was crying?
Probably a dream. It's just a phase
She's going through. I'll go to her.
You go to bed. I can't think
What's the matter with my head.
        There, there, the
Way you cry you'd think I was an
Awful sight. Now be a good girl,
Go to sleep. Good night.

Tiananmen Square
June 4, 1989

Karl Marx, take your time,
looming over Highgate on your plinth.
Snow's falling on your beard,
exiled, huge, hairy, genderless.

Terminally angry, piss-poor,
stuffed on utopias and cold,
cold as iron.

I'm thinking of your loving wife,
your desperate children and your grandchild
dead behind the barred enclosure of your brain.
Men's ideas the product, not the cause
of history, you said?

The snow has killed the lilacs.
Whose idea?
The air is frozen with theory.

What can the man be doing all day
in that cold place?
What can he be writing?
What can he be reading?
What big eyes you have, mama!
Next year, child, we will eat.

I'm thinking of my middle-class German grandmother
soft as a pigeon, who wept
when Chamberlain declared a war.
Why are you crying, grandma?
It's only the big bad wolf, my dear.
It's only a story.

There's no end to it.
The wolves have come again.
What shall I tell my grandchildren?

No end to the requiems, the burning trains,
the guns, the shouting in the streets,
the outraged stars, the anguished face
of terror under ragged headbands
soaked in death's calligraphy.

Don't turn your back, I'll say.
Look hard.
Move into that frozen swarming screen.
How far can you run with a bullet in your brain?

And forgive, if you can, the safety of a poem
sharpened on a grieving night.

A story has to start somewhere.

Soup and Jelly

'Feed Fred and sit with him
and mind he doesn't walk about.
He falls. Tell him his ute is safe
back home. Thinks someone's pinched it,
peers around the carpark all the time.
His family brought him in it and
he thinks it's gone.
He was a farmer once . . .'

I take the tray. The ice-cream's almost
melted round the crumbled orange jelly
and the soup's too hot. I know
I'll have to blow on it.

Hunched, trapped behind a tray,
he glances sideways, face as brown
and caverned as the land itself,
long thin lips droop ironic
at the corners, gaunt nose.
The blue and white pyjamas cage
the restless rangy legs.
In and out they go, the feet
in cotton socks feeling for the ground.

'Are you a foreigner?'
'Not exactly. Just a little sunburnt,'
and I put the jelly down. I mustn't feel
a thing: my smile has come unstuck.
I place a paper napkin on his lap. He winces.
'You're a foreigner all right,' he says.
'OK,' I say. What's one displacement more or less,
wishing I were a hearty flat-faced Fenian
with a perm and nothing doing in the belfry.
Someone like his mother. Or a wife who
spared him the sorrow of himself.
Now he grabs the spoon. 'I'll do it.'
'Right,' I say, 'You go ahead. Just ask me
if you want some help.' The tone's not right.
I watch the trembling progress of the spoon
for what seems years, paralysed with pity
for his pride.

How does a dark-faced woman give a man called Fred
who cropped a farm and drove a battered ute
a meal of soup and jelly?

Outside the window, clouds are swelling
into growing darkness and there's a man
hard on his knees planting something in the rain.

Jennifer Strauss

Report from the Mid-Century Mark

This is the year of fire and drought,
A terror out of childhood stalks my dreams.
The newspapers gabble of death, elections;
Promises and dead sheep
Bloat on front pages;
The barren clouds grow dark and swell
But drop no rain. Only there falls
From out of a clear sky
This new, this unexpected lover.
We burn, we melt for each other
Drinking champagne in bed
While the rose at my window parches.

I visit hastily in hospital
The friend of twenty years
Whose staring bones appall my solid flesh.
Her skin sheds in flakes. The ward's hot.
High in the wall, green-patterned glass
Is cool towards the old Greek woman
Who screams and screams
Because nobody answers her pain, her speech.
When my lover says 'Do you
Think of me? Do you think of me?'
My fingers smell of sweet flesh
But my tongue's ash dry.

The Snapshot Album of the Innocent Tourist

This is a space for the President's
Rather splendid Palace,
Standing above
The not-so-picturesque
Riverflat shanties.
'Prohibido!' said the baby-faced boy
Whose gun was real,
'Prohibido!': I got the message
If not the shot.

This is a space for the corner
Where the student was beaten to death
And for the feet of workers
Stepping, they said, at morning
Round a pool of blood.
I couldn't focus it
For Christmas traffic
And besides it looked
Like any intersection, anywhere.

This space is for twenty working years
Erased from the centre
Of a teacher's life.
'It's good to be back,' he says
And smiles as if believing
The text can be restored:
All its pages,
The ungiven lectures, the burnt books,
The silenced words.

This is a space for the disbelief
Of the elegant woman
Whose perfume is charming
Like her apartment.
Only the tiniest hairline scar
Betrays the facial tuck, the will to deny:
'It was terrible,' she cries
'But nobody knew. Nobody spoke.
How could we know?'

This space is for the grandparents
Who hid a dangerous child,
Unregistered,
Infected by his father,
Who died 'resisting arrest,' his mother
Who left for a meeting
And never came back,
Except in the set of his mouth
When the boy is angry, or laughs.

This is a space for all the disappeared
Who fade in other people's albums:
This is a space for courage
And for love,
For things that don't show up
In negatives.

A Mother's Day Letter: Not for Posting

When you were small you'd fall,
graze a knee, break a collar-bone,
nothing that could not be kissed
and mended—except the blow
death struck, we never spoke of.

I wanted you brave, concerned,
intelligent. Fifteen years late
you tell of fearing your dead
father's anger. What of my pride
that would not consider happiness

in the mere three wishes we get?
Swan-grown you ruffle your plumage
on history's polluted tide.
And I'm like any goose-girl now,
crying 'Come back! Come back!'

'The woods of love are wild
with beasts. In politics' swamp
your sinking feet will hit
toe-breaking boulders of stupidity,
strike razor edges of spite.'

No. Marshal the necessary march.
But if you come back shieldless,
remember I've no appetite for Spartan
deaths. I want you brave,
concerned, intelligent, alive.

Margaret Scott

From *Housework*

Polishing the Step

The front step's covered with a thin brass skin
that I polish up once in a blue moon,
washing it first, then wiping on clots
of Brasso that curdle to poisonous green
and rub off black until, if I keep at it,
a rippling jaundiced face with hang-dog eyes
looks up from a sheet of glint. But it won't last.
Settling fogs, salt-laden evening damps
will breathe it dull again in a week or two.
Earlier women had daily trysts with this step.
After cleaning the range and scrubbing the
white-wood table they'd kneel to meet
lugubrious reflections, queerer still
than those the world gave back—brazen hussy,
golden-hearted treasure. All lost, all gone.
The metal never admits to an old lie.
It's little wonder brass has a bad name,
impervious, blatant, lacking in charity,
or that poets, seeing their elbow-grease go
for nothing, their images fade,
write verses damning brass and sluttish time
and pin their faith on polishing a rhyme.

Doing the Washing

Wash days came to my mother surely as seasons.
Everything she used—copper, boiler-stick, mangle,
the chipped enamel bath that caught the drips,
the prop, the wicker basket—was heavy, awkward,
durable as the clumsy ploughs, the mattocks, scythes
and flails of labour in the old round of the fields.

Sometimes wind and rain got the better of her.
Sodden sheets were draped around the fire.
The day went down in steam and spoiled harvest.
But often, after the ironing had all been done
and the iron stowed in its place, the house
at evening smelled of well-aired linen,
gathered, folded, smoothed ready for use.
Up in the garden, pegging out drip-dry shirts
on a Sunday night, I feel rebuked by all
that dedication, that patient rhythmic toil.
I'm obsessed by omens, gambling by moonlight
on filling the outer lines of the Hill's hoist,
on finding the clothes add up to a given number.
A win can seem like something saved for the future,
chaos defeated again, a clean sheet.

Cleaning Windows

I don't much like cleaning windows. Ladders wobble.
You can get mugged by buckets. Upper windows
gleam when I'm twelve feet up but look worse
than before they were washed when I've clambered down.
You can see both sides at once—the liberal dilemma—
so it's often hard to decide what's splashed the glass—
soup or a passing bird. I feel watched by
opponents of aerosol cans, by consciousness-raisers,
by looming aproned figures from childhood,
by all those sparkling television girls
who show the smiling easy way to clean.
I can be brisk, keeping my mind on the job,
or switch my hand to on and watch the sky.
I can brood on reading the signs, on whether
it's healthier to reflect or concentrate.
In any case the smears show up at night
and there in the darkened glass that shape again,
that anti-heroine, that dismal clown with the
oh-so-predictable foot in a bucket of suds,
the yell from the teetering ladder, the comical angst.

Proteus

We spread the big red beach towel on the sand
and lay side by side in the sun—Proteus and I.
He propped himself on his elbow, Roman fashion,
one heavy wrinkled hand tangled in wet hair.
His coppery blue bulk, patched with glittering sand,
gleamed like a muscled map of new worlds.

He had risen at high noon from the quiet sea,
letting a cats-paw darken the water's face
to conceal his coming. Pouring weed,
crusted with shell and salt,
he'd stood in the shallows, counting his seals,
until I'd crept to his side and caught his hand.

His beard flared into mane. He showed his teeth.
My fingers scrabbled in coarse tawny hair,
on scales, in black fur.
He roared, hissed, snarled,
his eyes hot amber, jet and baleful green.
He fountained into a tree and fell as a breaking wave
then sighed in my dripping arms,
and promised out of his infinite fabled wisdom
to answer my pesky riddles of chance and change.

Yet as we lay in the flood of afternoon,
every moment together leaching away,
the great map re-shaping as he stirred,
no question came. I only watched
the glint of his streaming girdle dull and die
and the stain spread on the towel
like dark blood.

At sunset he smiled and ambled back to the sea.
The sun blinked its yellow eye.
Sand hissed in the dusk across the beach.
In his sliding torrent of seals
Proteus loomed for an instant like an oak.
His silence, his blue smile flowed
with our lion-gold hours to sleek night;
the moment bled away to father forth
new serpents, trees and tides
and all the oracular shapes of uncharted love.

A Walk on the Beach

Nothing but quiet air and the settling, breathing sound
of millions of tiny crabs, scattered like seed
over miles of puddled sand.
Soon I'll hear the scuff and flap of your thongs
cantering down the long slope to the beach.
As you come to find me here in the heel
of the bay, half-submerged in warmth among
littered shells and dry, whiskery weed,
my blood will rise to meet you like a wave.
If afterwards we walk out hand in hand
to the pale, flickering margin of the sea,
don't talk today — today at least — of the price
that's paid for such a simple freedom, of how
we could never stroll, leisured, well-fed,
in our tee-shirts from Taiwan, swinging my
woven Filipino beach-bag, unless half
the world suffered deprivation.
Don't say that if no-one's to go to bed
hungry, all this — what we have, what we are —
must utterly change.
No, not today, Let's walk in the soft air,
hands laced quietly together, our smooth bare
arms touching. Let's smile in each other's eyes
as the crabs writhe and splinter underfoot
in the long, murderous barrage of our tread.

Antigone Kefala

The Promised Land

I

The roads were of candy
the houses of ice-cream
the cattle of liquorice.
Pretty, we said,
drinking the green air,
as in a fairy tale, we said,

eating the green water, brackish,
breathing the smoke that rose
from the greenstone hills
and the moon alone
nailed at the bottom of the sky.

II

The people carved in wood
the mark of the knife still on them
a nordic dream whittled to knick-knacks
with glass beads in their sockets
which they washed every night
in detergents
to bleach away the weight
and travel light.

We, still walking on the high seas
drunk on the light
cobalt blue falling in tinselled drops
on the verdigris statue of the queen
stout, with a night cap on
and an orb.

III

In time
the rain closed in on us
the night like a black liquid
we fell in it
travelled down through the oil
drained of resonance
while they drank it away
in the tiled tombs
with the wingless birds on the walls
heraldic birds, with long monkey hair
and blind eyes.

IV

When our eyes failed
we used our hands
to finger the light
but the bones of the dead
were not there

eaten away by the wet
rising like breath from the leaves
the feathers of birds
a plumage the colour of mud.

Others before had read all
the signs and buried the magic
left only the wild grass
pushing bold everywhere.

V

At the tables
the plastic flowers marked by flies
and the cutlery limp
they were serving our marrow
with the boiled peas
chewing it patiently with their dentures
and singing
—for he's a jolly good fellow—

The spirits of the land
which they had slain
moved in their dreams
with eyes of burning coal
the thrust of wild beasts
coming at night with the full moon
to grip them by the throat
change the course of their appetites
give them strange diets.

Sunday Visit

We listened to the music,
carefully tracing the blue patterns
of the Persian rug.
Time waited, dusted, polished,
faded like the china cups.
Through the glass doors
the spring wind moved the trees;
unsettled wind,
unsure and full of boldness.

Another cup of coffee?
They had shrunk slightly
and their eyes looked dimmer.
The Greek in the next flat had died
during the winter, the poor man.
They still went for their walks,
had planted a new daphne by the wall,
watched the resilience of the new shoots
children's arms, firm, round,
shaded so slightly by blonde silky hair.
In the evenings
they returned to the old country.

Barbecue

At our back
the forbidden house
and beyond
the convent on the hill
massive red.

The streets deserted
only we in the bald yard,
with the gum tree
fanning itself nervously,
eating raw meat laced
with black flies
drinking the parched wind
and making polite conversation
while the light poured on us
sizzling.

Judith Rodriguez

Five Poems on Memory

Here you come, memory,
with your big bag.
Or is it me staggering
hauling the monster treasure?
Or me there inside?

(Just inside my boundaries
waits last year's woman,
behind my nose, her nose,
further inside, the schoolgirl
with her stained finger callus,
holding the baby, the oldest me, in the dark
like a wooden babushka.)

In a flash
St Elmo's fire, the portent,
touches the taut rigging,
strikes, streaks, leaps,
terrifies the sailors.

I wake up struggling with memory.
Tar and feathers, tar and feathers
stifle and stink and thicken
all over this *nincompoop*
schoolgirl shamed in class
over and over
all over again.

Sunlight is timing my days
but behind me the other light
shadows me, shows me
a dark manikin ahead.
I hurry with arms outstretched
to hold her hurrying
with arms outstretched
past the horizon.

Memory, my good dog, you eat up
the food I have set.
Then we go for a walk.
I have a path in mind;
you have your concerns.
Each course you set
by landmarks I can't discern
hauls at the walk we design
together.

Family

In my mother's family
We have no ancestors
only the long silence
between pogroms.

In my father's family
we have little tradition —
lands, legends, powers
passed us by.

In my country
we have no grandparents
no continuing song
no dances. Silence

feeds music,
father's our legend.
Husband and wife, estuary
into a continent,

we open our arms:
touch peaks, touch breakers.
Forest and white water
our children dance.

Mudcrab at Gambaro's

(For Tom Shapcott)

At Gambaro's, we are fearfully pleased
to light on land-agents in threes
and fours for lunch.
They check us for affluence
and return to their talk.
Well, and so the Big Boy's coming back —
did he tie it up?

Conducted, placed,
we toast the midday feast.
Morning's boom holds up,
zooms into the order of mudcrab.

You pour, you tumble
ice, you burrow the bottle. I tipple and wonder
how light's wine-colour.

The pallid easy oysters
pass, precursors
to here it comes! the roseate big 'un!
platefuls of plated pincers,
shanks, joints,
every one neatly smashed, our own Big Boy,
heaped up high.

We eat, ingenious and attentive.
The land-agents breathe heavily.
Among tables, through the room
grave women come
gathering greaves,
flanges, splinters we forced with hands bleeding—
devotees

of smooth encapsulated
flesh, the tingling white
of beachsand at daybreak.
Staggering, the land boys push back
their dogged chairs.
Mere steak. They diminish sweating in the late-lunch glare.
We are mudcrab, and air.

J. S. Harry

'the baby, with the bath-water, thrown out'

     :   it will not seem
     a meaningful exercise, to them,
     to hunt new life
     to stuff this particular cliche

     the small foetus
     already on its way

     through the grid
     at the bottom of the shower-alcove

even here   needing help
under water pressure
resistant
to being broken up

They will not meet again

Each pair of eyes
reminds the other
of an eyelessness

that joins them

Dropped   also by accident words
do not fall   with
an unborn's colour

Nor
do they need to be pushed

in quite the same way
to be allowed to fit

through a grating—
The shower-pipe leads straight to the main drain
which is mercifully silent
                              no acknowledgement
appropriate, for so small
a sac of blood

One of them will stay on
in the apartment

above it—
pale chook on a china egg
set to brood for a century

a shot of war

while those disintegrated by exocet
are unable to be present,
mrs thatcher—well wrapped
against the 'killing' chill

by a several foot
thickness of photographers
& 'fortified'
by the champagne-bubble-knowledge
that the war
was 'justified'—politically—
by being a success—in general—
with the british public—
&—in particular—
had improved
her popularity,
in january 1983
visits the falkland islands,
lays wreaths   on the ground
            above
'the british war-loss'—
& 'plays'
at being the one
to 'fire'
a military gun

a salon hair-do 's blown to pieces
by the force of the falkland gales
which, earlier, pushed up those seas
through which, on which, & under which
particular, british, & argentinian,
soldiers, sailors, & de-planed airmen
were struggling, freezing, & dying,
& she 'jumps' like an ordinary
first-time-soldier
pushed back   by the noise
& power of the gun

'kittenish'
behaviour drops from her
at this sound   so 'like'
a shot of war

underground the
recovered, drowned, burned, shot,
blown up, or frozen
are unable to oblige
by 'doing it again'
for the publicity picture

From *The Life on Water and the Life Beneath*

2

To remove vagueness is to outline the penumbra of a shadow.
The line is there after we have drawn it and not before.
Wittgenstein

When they'd finished
the dam to drown the valley, it had been summer.
Water gathered slowly, swelling first inside the river.
                              Once
the banks had been breached, there was no point
at which anyone could toss
an apple core and say, *Splash!*
That's the river. From splash-ripples out
the drowned valley starts. A vagueness
grew in people's minds. How could
any memory hold the line
of a water's silver
that had been already thickened
by the expansion of its own colour . . . No one
in his class had drawn it, the river, as it was.
No faithful, following, line of gums
played 'dog' to the river's 'drover'.
Gums
          were about,
                              some near
the river
              some not.

And, grey in winter, green in summer,
tippling constantly,
no convenient
line of drinker-willows
knelt, stumbled, leaned,
stood, or fell,
against their bar
that was the river.

The ford
had a pebble bottom.
Kids plashed there, after small
wet-eyed, leaf-bronze frogs,

as slim as pocket rubbers
and as droppable
and after stone collections, that slipped
and clinked, against one another
in your pockets.

The water-brilliance of the stones
that you took home
faded into dullness
before you could show a
mother father sister or a
brother.

Where is the music for the spread
of water's silence
over landscape. What is the sound
that will silk over your ears' skin
like the silence of water?

Chorus & Protagonists

Over
Centennial Park—
where Patrick White
used to walk—above
where he wanted
                    his ashes blent—
in the middle distance, black birds
flap & wrap themselves, as if
round invisible lumps of air. They look like
bits of coal-sheeny washing:
wind-caught undergarments from Greek tragedy.
Cah, they cry, they are both
chorus & protagonists, as they swoop & flap
their underclothes of death
low over the
small birds darting into the tea-tree thickets.

At dusk a different
conspicuous villain
sits in the huge fig, he is black
with a white-tipped tail, gold
rings round his eyes like a gypsy.

Casually swinging from the tip of his beak
like a silverblue sardine
he has stabbed from the blue
tin of the air, he holds, before taking up
to dismember, on the upper branch,
before the student-audience, his three
gawky ignorant fledglings,
one perfect
Dusky Wood Swallow.
The class is Dismemberment 1 (Life-Drama)
for about-to-graduate Currawongs.

Kate Llewellyn

Peri's Farm

(For Jerry Rogers)

Occasionally even though it's winter
the mango plops a fruit down
Peri makes her breakfast of it

white fan-tail pigeons strut
blue and orange parrots flutter
above the yellow vine

the rain pours down heavy as wax

the butcher bird
sings its heart out daily
on the white verandah rail

'That's me' says Peri
'its name is Merle in French'

so who's that thick and sensuous
carpet snake
curled up in the eaves above the bird tray
Peri names him too
and has him delicately removed
to where he'll do no harm

we eat prawns and octopus
on the wide verandah
the hammock sags and waits

the rain pours down like wax

at night we light the candles
play gorgeous gloomy tunes
and plan our lavish funerals

Peri drinks a whisky sour
I stay on the wine

the green frog a pulsing emerald
appears in the bathroom as a prince
'I know who he is too' she says
and whispers me his name

and still down comes the rain

she says 'I'm so frustrated
I could kick the door down'

'That is the condition
under which many of us live' say I

my iron bed has Justin's saddle
hanging on the end
the french windows are open wide

the rain pours down like honey

wind and lightning whip the plants
shiny and tormented
some are rooted out

the river breaks its banks
the house becomes surrounded
'Don't worry' Peri says
'I've had it all re-stumped
there's a new tin roof
we can last for days'

the rain pours down like wax

cattle float and with them goes a man
the billabong goes out
to meet the river
like a bride
ibis fly like medieval emblems

the gleaming ostentatious rooster
strides around the garden
'I know who he is too
he flew here when my mother died
there's her grave
it's in the flower bed
see she overlooks the river
she always liked that view'

there's a curved brown plait of bread
left on the kitchen step
it makes a basket holding six warm muffins

even if we can't have what we want
at least we've got simple human kindness

the rain pours down like wax

so what if I'm reduced
to writing erotic letters
I never plan to post

Peri writes all the parts of the body
down in French
it limbers up her mind

the rain stops for an hour or so
she goes swimming in the estuary
later we find out it holds
two white pointer sharks

the rare tropical fruit trees
the bougainvillea
and the washing sag above the flood

the waters keep on rising
'We'll need that ark you wanted
as your vessel—see where your games
and talk have got us' says Peri

I squeeze another grapefruit
and pass her whisky sour
she walks around in black and shiny bathers
with something on her mind
I tell her what the secret was
'How did you know?
I didn't know myself'

'Your body knew' I said
'it was that that told me'

'When does it ever end?'
I ask

'Will it never?
will we both be banging on the coffin lid
crying *Oh love me one more time*
while our limbs cool and set like wax'

Jan Owen

This Marriage

The Well

After the angel had been
and her father's first anger was done,
she left her mother wringing
a chicken's neck, tight-lipped,
and sank down by the courtyard vine
and felt her gorge rise up.
She had half-forgotten the light.
Here, only her queasy heart
like a flapping wing,
hens'-down filling the air
with a warm bird smell,
and the dull weight at her core.
She leant on the trunk of the vine,
hard as the sinews of her fathers,
till the sickness passed
then pulled herself up
and took the two buckets —
the new one Joseph had made

and the rickety one
with the handle worn.
On the path to the well,
the fallen olives
purpled her sandals with their stain.

Straw

Joseph stayed unsure
in spite of the dream.
When the pains began she was calm
as the oxen in their stalls
who shifted and sighed and knew.
He was afraid. This was woman's work. Somehow
he got a fire going and had some water warm.
In the end it was easier than he thought,
the boy slipped into his hands
neat as a trout
and blinked at the stable's dim gold world.
He washed and swaddled him
and put him to Mary's breast.
Then remembered the afterbirth
in the straw somewhere
and carried it out and fed the fire.
He was washing his hands with snow
when the shepherds came,
two dumbstruck men and a boy with a lamb,
a gift, they said, for the newborn lord,
wiping away all doubt
with this odd hurt—
the heavenly hosts had not appeared to him.
He bowed his head and led the strangers in.

The Blue Gown

And when the time had elapsed
and the day come
that he might go to her,
she rubbed myrrh on her throat,
touched cinnamon to her tongue,
and hung between her breasts
a silver amulet of snakes entwined
then lit three candles on a low pine stool
and loosened the string
of the gown her mother stitched
against this night.

He drew aside the brocade,
standing a little uncertain,
a quiet stranger
who'd washed her bloodied thighs
and seen her milk well up.
She let her gown slip to a pool,
in duty and gratitude she would have said.
But when he drew his clothes off awkwardly
and she saw him for the first time,
quite unexpectedly she ran and knelt
and pressed her cheek to his skin
and circled him with her arms.
His hardness at her bosom and neck
was a curious creature
she could rouse and tame
now that her body was her own.
His hands like promises
were lifting her hair.

Leaves

It was bright moonlight.
In another room the boy awoke
and quietly lay and sucked his fist.
He heard a night-bird call,
the scritch of a beetle,
and scrabble of a mouse.
He could not know yet who he was
but watched the fig-tree cast
its pattern on an inner wall
and studied the light and shadow
in his father's house.

The Pomegranate Tree

The second time,
a midwife hustled the man
straight out into the yard.
He sat in the shed
with the planed wood round his feet
and the shavings' tight blond curls
till the woman's triumphant shrill.
When Mary was asleep
he took the child up in his coat
doubled against the wind

and went out to the pomegranate
heavy with open fruit
and watched the sun go down,
bending his head to catch
the sure breath of this infant,
mortal and his own.

Jennifer Rankin

Forever the Snake

Awkward on a hillock of grass
feet falling forward over the edge
cramped close to the children
away from the snake.

And in that patch of long reed it is waiting.

You pick up a spade.
Eyes pace out the ground.
Your left hand is clenched on itself
nails bite into your skin.

A heavy grey rock lies in the reeds.
With one move you upend it.
The children edge closer on the hilly rise
they stand on my feet.

I see you consider and bend
you probe with the spade.

And then it is here.

Snake. Flashing its back
arrowing through grass
black missile with small guiding head
firing off reflexes, straight into attack.

And the spade. Lifeless and foreign
under your hand raised in the air.

This black speeding nerve is cutting through space.

Somewhere forever your hand is raised
in far-off space fields the snake is racing.

Now the thick spade crashes down from above
snapping the nerve that even in death sends its messages.

We inch about on our hillock of earth.
The back of the snake is still thrashing.
You stand with its head under your spade
you are locked to its spine.

Far-out in space the snake is still speeding
rushing through grass to attack.

Closer in space the spade has been raised.

Here on the grass the black nerve is broken.

Yet always the snake is now striking
in the quiet, in the space beyond time.

Song

Wash the air with voices tonight
and I will be carried away
traveling quite slowly
on Razorback Mountain.

Record the sound of the old
Hudson Terraplane
—girl, thats our car—
glide gently past mornings of drought
and on into good Royal Show years.
Stop at the top for the view.

One day he became a delinquent
simply like that
she went away with a doctor
ran off the road in no gear.
Those left brought some solace to dwell on
counting the sheep every trip.

Tonight twist the wire quite tightly
over the gate
and wait while I make
the round journey
once more on Razorback Mountain.

Love Affair 36

On the seventh day

in the late afternoon
with shadow already entering the valley

I watched your biceps.

They were flashing and beeping.
They were signaling confidence.

And I knew that my eyes were darkening
I knew that my eyes were slits when I glanced

as you walked on the balls of your feet through that house

your hips quite taut below your brain
and your lips too sweet by far.

And I stayed behind in the bedroom.

I was tossing and turning
I was considering the stars
I was laconically flicking a page
I was reading the dictionary
I was brushing my hair
I was wrapping myself in a shroud.

I lay on the bed with my terrible eye
and you strutted outside the door.

I ate a crisp apple
bursting the skin with my teeth.

You whistled so lightly in the bathroom
I very nearly stabbed you there
blood all over the green-tiled floor

toothpaste in your beard
a smile on your lips
apple between my teeth.

Instead I slowly turned the page
and the paper smelt of ink and a summer breeze.

Old Currawong

After the sudden rain
the heavy after-drops still thudding

a large black currawong slipping
gripping rasping in the corrugations of the iron roof

and the lorikeets flying in only as colour
and the talking of the koels and the crows circling above

I see the black neck stretching
the opening beak the awkward sliding feet

always unbalancing trying to regain to stand up straight

while the great heavy weight of the body
slips on and over the roof

The last of the rain falls hard and separate and of its own

But the beak of the bird is still there high on the roof.

Yes the beak is still there pinned to the iron ridge.

I see it open I see the long dark shaft of the beak open

From deep below the earth it pulls out its cry.

Lee Cataldi

the dressing shed

on the notice
nude sunbaking
prohibited is obliterated

no doors on the cubicles

the seats have their own tiled rooves
like post-war plastic children's toys

the showers
pour down from a great height
like the sun

warm sheltered deserted

here a hundred women once
with perfect modesty
donned bathing suits

now one lone englishwoman
in a bathrobe and wedgies
does ballet school exercises

Neilsen Park
the evening sun
bursts like a bomb on Centrepoint

illegal dogs and bicycles come out
afterwork swimmers thrash by
the buzz of outboard motors in their ears

all day
old people drift with the tide
along a line of sand
their eyes absorbing more and more of the green
and dim qualities of water

beached
like the bleached skeleton of a dead whale
the dressing shed

harbours insects and memories
fading like photographs
of picnics and weddings

quiet

at night
through alien trees
their unnaturally shiny leaves
still holding the sun
the soft sea breeze
with its acrid foreign smell
breaks through curtain and mosquito net
dissolving illusions of gable and stone
illusions of home

busily in the dressing shed
termite and dry rot
reduce its bones to ashes
the ant picks over the remains
grass sprouts through the concrete

the abandoned clothes
of bathers passed on into anecdote
pile up inside the wire enclosure
we are forbidden to enter

a jumbled memorial

kuukuu kardiya *and the women who live on the ground*

1

australian museum october 1982

behind the microphone
pale face and hair
I was almost sure sitting
in the same row of desks for ten years
one doesn't forget
the toss of the head

femmocrat
black and gold dress gold
handbag fat
as a bank account

meanwhile
in the draughty hall
the Warlpiri women wait
their painted breasts
delicate as earth

and into
the mismanaged white festival
miraculous and powerful
quavering
fine harmonies the certain
feathery presences

the artists stop
discuss a point of style the song
continues it is
a continuum   sometimes
they sing it aloud

the women move lightly   brown
skin black skirts in a ring
like a windbreak
                            at dawn blue
smoke from cooking fires bodies
stirring in blankets a warm
outcrop of earth

2

the white woman
comes out of the house she says
        wash the clothes
        finish the job   wipe
        the children's noses we are
        taking these children away
        it's for their own good

the women who live on the ground
disappear into the desert
stepping lightly
out of their regulation mission bloomers
their ragged jumble sale clothing

their voices fade as water
sinks back underground

jukurra jukurra they say
taking their children with them

into the heart of that furnace
where spirits rise whiter than clay

3

the women are in the school
with the children who
are learning to read
yirdi they say
wirlinyirnalu yanu marluku
we went hunting for kangaroo
walyangka karnalu nyina
we live on the ground

the white woman
riding her mop like a broomstick
screams about the building
            what a waste of time   they should be
            learning to spell must and ought
            they are filthy   look
            at their noses   look
            at the dust on the floor   look
            at the dust on the ground

outside the school the children
write *warlpiri* in the dust write
kuukuu kardiya in the dust the hot wind
blows into eyes throats noses
into all the clean clothes

the women who live on the ground
watch the white women fade
after a few years
back into their motor cars
after one or two of these seasons in which
the spirits of the secret places
open their giant lungs
and burn the houses to ash

your body

your body is on
the tip of my tongue

your entire physiology is on
the tip of my tongue
your personal and social history
your psychology
your metaphysic and the structure
of your phantasy system are on

the tip of my tongue

your family
your relatives near and distant
by blood or marriage
the places you've been
the movies you've seen
the houses and apartments you have inhabited
are all
now on
the tip of my tongue

sometimes I imagine
our souls
the way nameless and formless
the tidal wave
ebbing and flowing under the universe
god
the spirits of our ancestors
the holy trinity are on
the tip of my tongue

alas
I do not have
the federal government
the financial times
queensland
shell oil
the royal family
the pentagon or any other
thing it would be better
to obliterate with a lick
of the lips on the tip

of my tongue

Wendy Poussard

Boston Tea Party

Today we climb the gates
into Pine Gap. Facilities
are nicer here, in some respects,
than in the dust outside . . .
green lawns, for instance
and a pool for birds.

Women with parasols
take tea and sandwiches
and stroll across the hills
like citizens of Boston, long ago
who would not pay for
other countries' wars.

One hundred and eleven
are arrested. The party's over.
A careful policeman empties out the pool
in case of germs.
Humans, a fragile species, lack
a balanced sense of danger.

Caroline Caddy

Frank

i

Ma locked us out.
She'd say dont come back till I call you.
We'd hang about—
steal a loaf of bread from the stands.
Then my brother got killed.
He used to wait for me at the corner.
When I got there this crowd of people told me
some kid got killed by a truck.
I finally found out it was my brother.

I had lots of fights.
I had this thing on body building.
I used to work out in this basement.
There was a girl   cousin I think
and some wedding going on upstairs.
I never had a girl.
I didnt want to ruin my strength   anyway
somehow I finished up on top of her.

ii

On manoeuvres they'd drop these flour bombs
then go round and say   you're dead   you're dead
you're dead   and you'd say OK.

We had to wade through water up this beach.
We tried to dig into the ground
but it wouldnt open up.
We were scared shitless all the time.
In this village it was weird   smoke still coming up
and people pushing wheelbarrows with wooden wheels.
We couldnt understand nothing.
There was this guy they reckoned killed a jew
so we beat shit out of him.
One guy in our outfit   if he wanted something
he just took   beat kill or whatever.
Like he was cold so he'd burn down a house
and these Germans jumping about and waving their arms.
We laughed.
Of course I knew you shouldnt do those things for
nothing.
He didnt care.
Not like me.
What I did was for taking my revenge.

Foreign Aid

All of you countries
        rich in catastrophes
                            send us your angels of death
to hunt mercifully down our needless streets
                                    and dump
Boeing-loads of Azerbaijan   Bangladesh.

Lend us full blown reason and cause—
                    a definite havoc on our embroiled
but havocless roofs.
Neutrally   naturally
            break the front yard marriages of trees
                        unslot foundations
so this wall we've been building
                    two bricks up one down for years
will be collapsed—
        cave-in completed so we can rise
                        shedding damage
armoured together against insurmountable odds
                        or at last against
each other.
I see no darkness overhead.
The land is too stable
                no give under the sun's long bolts.
For all our skin to skin attempts at merger
                        love goes out
like foreign aid—
I don't want to be you but I want you to be like . . .
Is this shadow
            or brightness that comes into me
                        when I imagine
you thrust suddenly towards the precipice
                    till you only want
                            to live
before it's too late
        all you oppressed by too many acts of gods
glide your long shapes over us
            so we can look up aghast
                        with relief.
In the clearblocks of night
                    we sweat in our own
designer black deaths—
                can't welcome
                        or ward off
ourselves.
The disaster is
            that we want to continue
                        to love.

Joanne Burns

genetics

men in suits during heatwaves
men in suits being cologne cool in heatwaves
men in suits walking with precision in heatwaves
men in suits wearing distinguished ties in heatwaves
men in suits with tight collars in heatwaves
men in suits whose buttocks protrude militarily
            when their collars are too tight in heatwaves
men in suits with firm jaws in heatwaves
men in suits with neat attache cases in heatwaves
men in suits with properly folded handkerchiefs in heatwaves
men in suits who wipe their brows discreetly in heatwaves
men in suits who never yell at their secretaries in heatwaves
men in suits who have dry handshakes in heatwaves
men in suits whose perfect wives are no less perfect in heatwaves
men in suits who would read ayn rand, omni, fortune etc. to
            optimize those periods of insomnia that may occur
            in heatwaves
sons of men in suits flamboyantly confident in designer shorts in
            heatwaves
sons of men in suits obstructing the movements of pedestrians
            with their defiantly raucous skateboards in heatwaves
sons of men in suits rolling forward towards those days when
            they will become men in suits allowing nothing to
            get in their way : undeterred by any kind of weather

lung lexicon

i

cardin (that's pierre) lays 'the soul of north africa' across your
living room floor with his carpet design. jog. jog.

ii

a travelling cosmetician says he has reached the point where
japan 'is a comfortable fact'

iii

in the last sydney to t-shirt surf race a nine year old runs up for a
drink, waves to the crowd, wearing 'autism in action' on her back.
the army boys sweat 'train hard, fight easy' on theirs. everyone
cheers. who says t.v. is killing literacy

iv

someone celebrates antarctica and the ex-p.o.w. reunion, both
1981, on the same garment

v

and a film critic writes of 'gallipoli' every human being is an event

vi

a popular monthly magazine centrefolds 'fashion for the nuclear
war' titled 'going out in style'

vii

there's a new sweatshirt in upper sydney bearing '100% physical'
in several scripts

viii

a mathematican who loses a wife, writes to the paper for
another, sharing compatible
                    holistic
                    orgasmic
                    familial
                    tribal
                    planetary
                    environmental
                    confluential
                    synergistic
                              outlooks/vistas/visions
                    he doesn't mention clothing
100% mental?
          GOTCHA

conviction: a transcript

i want to share with you a fabulous new range of saucepans: each individual pan is of course marvellous but this one is simply the most marvellous because of its wonderful glass lid: see the gorgeous little spatchcocks cooking away: it's so exciting to see the things watching: that is i mean anyway: this pan will cook right through the creatures: they're very strong and handsome: there's a lifetime guarantee and you don't have to buy the whole range all at once: you can build them up up and up: we'll be talking about your immune system followed by the ageing of the neck after these messages from our sponsors: stay tuned: and tomorrow in the studio we'll have one of our most popular graphic designers speaking of the fresh boost of inspiration he got from a recent tour of famine torn pockets of africa: while leading fashion consultants will give advice on your investment wardrobe: colour, cut, coordinates: how to get that optimum yield

Alison Clark

Incipit Vita Nova (Again)

(For Helen)

In a strange city you want
not to miss a trick: read all the signs
with an open mind, trying as in a mirror
to catch the look before expression sets.

Eating sandwiches on the grass
with someone who is almost silent, you ask:
Is it the natural condition of the soul
to suffer? His mild experienced 'Yes'.

But it seems a quarter-centimetre twist
of the perspective on (not all of) our sorrows
might cast the prismatic
light of quiet cathedrals.

You roam city and country
trying to get it right, to learn the tactic.
But oh, those exacting labels in the Botanic Gardens!
If I forget *Potentilla fruticosa* is it serious?

Reclaiming the Feminine

At the Catholic conference
a soupy lady sang a chorus
and the one thanking the speaker
had to wait for two more verses . . .

Meanwhile back at the opera
the big virgin in her satin tent
(paradigm for the sex that loves
and trills) grieves for her little tenor

who's fled, helping the captive queen
disguised in his love's
bridal veil. Brain fever!
She—trailing posies, left

like a large white wedding cake
no-one will eat, mound
of obsessive flesh in a male
world of swords and rhetoric—

needs the quiet figure on the rostrum
urging her congregation
to bring the dark, feeling god
forward into the light.

Diane Fahey

The Pool

He has given her this room of mirrors, in which she is bored;
she may speak to him only when he speaks to her.

He spends most of his time by the pool. What is it he sees,
staring down at its tiled floor—some classical coin

with shimmering bronze face? He is as beautiful as a dolphin
but never swims. She often does. She likes the splashing cry

of the water as her long arms slice through vivid green.
Why does he never look at her? He is always looking down—

even into his glass as they sit in the evening by the pool.
'Have you had a nice day?' (he stirs and pokes his ice);

'. . . a nice day?' she echoes, desolate.
                                        Oh, but she loves him!
Once she swam the pool's whole length to surprise him,

curving up to where he gazed soulfully, teardrops pocking
the chlorine. At first he did not see her face, then,

when she was almost out of breath—but still smiling—
those clear eyes glazed with shock and he looked away.

She did not hear the slapping of her feet on concrete
as she walked inside then dripped up the long, soft stairs

to her room. 'With only mirrors to keep me company
I shall waste away, waste away . . .' she thought,

but could not say—as usual, the words stuck in her throat.
And she curled into herself, hiding from all those faces.

Stretched out flat by the pool, he too loved and wasted,
had not even sensed her walking away, her stifled sigh.

The Chinese Astronomer

A Chinese astronomer sits opposite me
at a breakfast table in Florence.
He has come from a conference in Trieste.
For two years he has lived in Switzerland.
Something or someone sent him there
and will decide when he goes back
to his wife and his son
who is about to enter Beijing University.
Perhaps he'll return by the end of the year?
I tell him I have been to Padua
and seen an observatory there
that Galileo must have used.
So many stairs, so many stars . . .

Later that day, he stumbles towards me
in the street, lost and in panic.
'Can you help me?' he pleads,
as if to a stranger,
expecting not to be understood.

That evening across the table,
conversation is difficult,
because he has drunk much,
and I have drunk nothing . . .
We speak different varieties
of perfect English, mention cities
as if they were bubbles or stars:
Amsterdam. Venice. London. Madrid.

Towards midnight,
re-entering my room,
I turn and catch, from the corridor's end,
his fugitive glance
in which despair outstrips all desire,
as if I were the phantom of his wife
destined always to pause at a threshold
then disappear into an unknown room.

At the beginning of the day,
in one of the pauses that was the conversation,
he had said, clearly, brokenly,
                              It is too long.
Then his hands had knocked over the sugar bowl—
white glistening mounds on a white tablecloth
that must have seemed as meaningless
as a map of the earth, or of the heavens.

Dressmaker

As a girl I loved fabrics, stitching and moulding them
to fit. I remember a flared dress, pink roses on white.
Wearing it with my first high heels, I tottered past
neighbourhood louts slung on a verandah;
                              from their transistor
Marty Robbins sang, 'A White Sport Coat
                              and a Pink Carnation'.

As I blushed, they eyed the smoky summer air.
                                        At sixteen,
a slippery silk dress with whorls of red and crimson,
pinched in with a cummerbund. With unswerving hips
I passed the greengrocer, an Italian who sighed, whistled,
called in one sound, his pregnant wife thrusting beans
and tomatoes into brown paper bags; her look touched mine:
wary, beyond challenge, sisterly.
                            Ten years of illness next,
when I bundled myself inside coats in summer, wore black
as often as not. Hard to stand straight inside a body
so out of kilter.
                Since then I have put on the garment
of my womanhood. It marks the curves and leanings
of my flesh, holds in, reveals, what I have come to be,
beyond promise and blight. I know its weight,
                                        its transparency,
its rawness, its flawed smoothness. I wear it now
with something close to ease, with the freedom, almost,
of nakedness.

Bobbi Sykes

Monopoly

The trip to England is a mighty success,
                    rah, rah, rah,
Militant Black Leader ARRIVES screams the Press;
Cold, wet, ugly, sprawling, grey
                    London,
Never mind the view—it's work you're here to do!

Railway stations, strange faces,
Performing black doll alights,
Here's the platform—
Talk, doll; rage, doll; rant, doll;
Horrors in Australia,
                    rah, rah, rah,
Tell it like it is, tell it like it is.

From home the news—
     'Police are out to get you'
     'Blacks are out to get you'
     'Whore, prostitute, deserter of children'
     'Wealthy, posing as poor'
     'Poor, posing as wealthy'
     'Left-wing communist extremist'
     'Counter-revolutionary, opportunist, elitist'

The cry rings in my ears,
     Paul Coe, Denis Walker,
     Gary Williams, Norma Williams,
     Gary Foley, Billy Craigie,
     Lyn Thompson—
     collective voices:
          'We are discriminated against because we are black!'

Quietly now—
     Bobbi Sykes is not as black as us,
               white as us,
               poor as us,
     Let us discriminate because we think she is
          'not the right kind of Black'.

Back to the platform—
Talk, doll; dance, doll;
Tears on black doll's face,
          rah, rah, rah,
Emote, doll, 'tis a sad tale of starvation and hunger that you tell
          and tell well.

Blacks in Australia need money to combat starvation, malnutrition,
          (Whore, prostitute,)
We have been beaten into the grass by the Government fascist pigs,
          (Deserter of children,)
We need help from abroad—
          (Wealthy, posing as poor,)
We appeal to people around the globe to rally to our aid.
          (Poor, posing as wealthy.)

Police victimization is acute,
          (Left wing extremist,)
Our country sisters are raped by white stockmen,
          (Counter-revolutionary,)
For political action on just claims we are flung into gaol,
          (Opportunist,)

The Government oppresses the people.
              (Elitist.)

Tears on black doll's face,
                    rah, rah, rah,
Cry, sister, tell it like it is!
Is the sorrow for the head-lice on the babies heads
        And children in rubbish bins in Alice?
Or for the knife which protrudes from your back?

Blacks have no monopoly on pain,
For within a black group an un-black black doll
Writhes, hurts, screams, cries out—
In soundless agony,
A hand at the throat blocks off the sound,
A black hand,
                    rah, rah, rah.

In slow motion in a troubled mind,
        Token nigger, spit on her,
        Uppity nigger, slap her down,
        Cheeky nigger, don't play with her,
        Faces of attackers—clear, then waning,
        Black and white faces, taut and straining.

White groups huddled over candles,
Playing games with life and riches,
Black doll knocking on the door,
'Let her in, she will amuse us',
Talk, doll; rave, doll; rant, doll;
                    rah, rah, rah.

Black group huddled in the night,
Making decisions which must be right,
Black doll knocking on the door,
'Let me in, let me help',
Go away, un-black black,
Only black blacks can help.

There is no monopoly on discrimination,
There is no monopoly on pain!
Play it one more time, black doll,
This time with tears,
                    rah, rah, rah.

Fallin'

The Sister has been raped, they said.

I squeezed my eyes tight-shut—in horror,
though I knew, knew, knew, that the horror had just begun;
In shock, but not in disbelief, I heard,
                    by five Brothers.

And I thought
Brother, flesh of my flesh,
You have watched / while we / your sisters
cried, gave birth, died, went insane, tore out our own hair,
spat on our own bodies, screamed the soundless scream,
sweated blood—
in agonies which white men caused, damn them and their lives

Yet you have still learned from them
and turn your new craft to us. Rape Bash Kill.

We, your Sisters, newly learnt
that protection is possible,
that with you by our side we are safe,
that together, we are all safe,
must learn again . . .

Must learn to defend ourselves
from those who stand so close,
eat of our table, of food which *we* prepared,
must learn again to recognize the mad-dog disease
which is again the white man's legacy.

One Day

        Moving along Main St. /
                Whitesville /
        Digging all them white faces /
                (Staring, or 'not staring')
        Until I felt surrounded /
                Lost / bobbing on a sea I didn't know /
        I began to concentrate so hard /
                (Head down)
        On the lines and cracks
                Of the footpath . . . .

And I felt you / unknown Brother /
        Across the street /
Over the heads / cars /
        Throwing me your glance /
Your salute / clenched fist /
        Smile . . . .

Fellow Black /
        You were majestic /
Your sparks lit up the street /
        Whitesville /
And I was no longer moving along /
        But / Brother
                Moving up!

Black Woman

Black Woman

    your near meat-less stew
    boils over in the kitchen
    you stand at the front door
    your baby in your arms
    next youngest twisting at your skirts
    you listen to the man
    from the Australia Party
    asking you to become a candidate
    in the forthcoming election
    —in your hand today's mail
    advising you of scholarship benefits
    and black medical services
    your mind wanders to johnny
    lying in the back room
    wheezing his tiny life away
    and to the two you lost before
    the advent of black services

Black Woman

    the electricity bill is not paid
    but the churches now court your attention
    you are asked to speak to groups
    in your st. vincent de paul dress
    but all the attention paid
    to your mate serving
    his ninth prison sentence

for breaking and entering the homes
of whites in the dead of night
to gather crumbs
to bring to your poor home
does not set him free
or put him back in your arms
nor let you look into his eyes
for one minute longer than 'visiting hours'.

Black Woman

the present is so un-real
its new *l*-liberal views
mouthing anti-racist slogans
in demonstrations of the day—
attempting to solicit your sexual favour
for a dollar and a drink
in the cold reality of night
you wonder if you were better off
before the trendy 70's
when you could stir your meatless stew
think of wheezing johnny
the un-paid bills
without interruptions from the new world
that promises much but delivers little

Black Woman

the tears you cry—you are told—
should be tears of joy
black women are on the way '*up*'
you now must ponder
who will babysit the kids
while you make your (un-paid) t.v. appearance
you must try not to let your bitterness
be construed as 'black racism'
as you recall the abuses
heaped upon you all your life
and you view your 'liberation'
with a scepticism born of poverty,
corrugated-iron shacks, no water,
four children from six live births
and the accumulated pain of two centuries

black woman black woman black woman black woman black

Lily Brett

The Excrement Cart

On the twenty-fifth
of every month
the excrement cart
came into your neighbourhood

two men or women
pulled the wagon
from the front
and two pushed at the back

the smell thickened the air
for hours before
these out-house emptiers
reached Palacowa street

by the time
the rickety cylindrical vehicle
arrived
it was almost overflowing

its contents
lurched over the sides
at every
upraised cobblestone

leaving
an abstract ochre
clotted trail
along Palacowa street

there was no shortage
of volunteers
for the career
of 'fekalist'

the position
carried
extra rations
of bread and soup

sometimes
families
worked
these wagons

the children
could hardly hold
the long-handled ladle
that was used as a scoop

the fekalists looked
more worn
more drawn
more sickly

and after a few months
they retired
with
tubercular lungs

sometimes
one
of them
survived

one evening
in
Melbourne
you introduced me

to Regina Kindler
a small woman
with oddly effervescent
hair

while she was chatting
she dabbed perfume
from a small silver bottle
behind her ears

on the back
of her wrists
between her breasts
on her neck

she dabbed
and dabbed
with quick
flicking gestures

poor Regina
you said
to me
later

sometimes
one
of them
survived.

Poland

What do you want
to go to Poland for
you screamed

your golden face
frozen
and distorted

the Poles
were worse
than the Germans

small children
in the towns around
the camp

would kick us
when we walked to work
in our striped rags

grown men
would throw
a piece of bread

and
nearly die with laughter
while we fought each other

oh
those nice Poles
those good people

what do you want
to go to Poland for
you wept

they
won't let you leave
so easily

something
terrible
will happen

Liebala Liebala
please
why go

you know
after the war
there was a miracle

not
one Pole
did know

about
what happened
to us

you
could smell
the flesh

burning
for
kilometres

the sky
was red
day and night

and
the Poles
didn't notice

Liebala Liebala
please
don't go.

Jeri Kroll

The Towers of Silence

Bombay

i   *The Parsees*

The shadows circle back and out of sight.
Below, the priest unlocks the park.
The dead above lie open to the light.

The relatives have spent the night
listening to the dogs of memory bark.
The shadows circle back and out of sight.

The Parsees bury brief, they slight
the sleepless worm, the quick, efficient spark.
The dead above lie open to the light.

Keep earth and fire pure. It's right
to strip the soul to sail up to the ark.
The shadows circle back and out of sight.

Keep good and evil pure. Their flight
from Persia kept them choosing: light or dark.
The dead above lie open to the light.

The Towers silence vultures' wings. Their height
echoes with the skeleton's remark.
The shadows circle back and out of sight.
The dead above lie open to the light.

ii *The Tourists*

Outside the circle of the park,
beyond the meditating few who mourn the light
gone from someone's eyes, who choose the right
path home, while the soul alone embarks
on its journey: flesh gone, skeleton in flight
down the tower's well into the round, small dark—

Outside the buses shudder, the ribbed dogs bark,
the tourists climb on, crane for their last sight
of forbidden shadows. A strange sensation. The height
of the towers seems to rise as the buses fight
down through taxis, scooters, cows, girls in tight
western jeans who stop traffic. They might
look round then: several Hindus, a Greek patriarch,
an English couple, Muslims with stark
eyes above their veils, the Japanese slight
and neat as ever. Everyone's eyes bright
from the smoke circling through. The vendors spark
the day: chappatis, dosa, rose and white
halva. Rich as beggars in the night,
the senses search much later through the dark
bazaars for something worth it in the smoky light.

Susan Afterman

Grandmother

She asks me to zip her dress.
She asks me not to vote Labor.
The cigarette-holder clicks between her teeth.
I close the double doors into the dining room,
we eat asparagus
beside christmas lilies erect in vases,
glass eggs on the sideboard emanating light.

The passionfruit vine roots deeper
into the bullock's heart she fed it.
In the glass-house maidenhair
ferns uncurl like nostrils
virgin moss-net, veils on veils
and spotted orchids furl their tails.

By the fire we clink our whiskey, ice and crystal;
dove-scraping on the roof sounds like her cough.
Pale feathers float down past the window
like the soft flesh of her arm
that melts between my fingers when I lift her.

Soldier Boy

Kangaroo lies dead by the road.
Smiles, bloated, like a soldier boy
in river lilies.
The fur stops the rot.
His big belly won't burst for a while.
I had a bloated belly, white skinned;
full of food, excrement
my bloody first son.
My belly burst and drained away,
I bled and flowed
a fetid river.

Kangaroo cries as his bowels are chewed out
shot through the startled eye.

Rhyll McMaster

Profiles of my Father

I

The night we went to see the Brisbane River
break its banks
my mother from her kitchen corner
stood on one foot and wailed, 'Oh Bill,
it's *dangerous*.'
'Darl,' my father reasoned,
'don't be Uncle Willy,'

And took me right down to the edge
at South Brisbane, near the Gasworks,
the Austin's small insignia winking
in the rain.

A policeman helped a man load
a mattress on his truck.
At a white railing we saw the brown water
boil off into the dark.
It rolled midstream higher than its banks
and people cheered when a cat on a crate,
and a white fridge whizzed past.

II

Every summer morning at five-thirty in the dark
I rummaged for my swimming bag
among musty gym shoes and Mum's hats from 1940
in the brown hall cupboard.

And Dad and I purred down through the sweet, fresh morning
still cool, but getting rosy
at Paul's Ice Cream factory,
and turned left at the Gasworks for South Brisbane Baths.

The day I was knocked off my kickboard
by an aspiring Olympian aged ten
it was cool and quiet and green down on the bottom.
Above in the swaying ceiling limbs like pink logs,
and knifing arms churned past.

From *My Mother and I Become Victims of a Stroke*

Residues

Her brain is stripped
to its inessentials.
She's disposed of the gears.
Her mind is full of old shoes
that don't fit.
Clothes. Which? Which?
She twitches a pair of slacks
over her shoulders.
'I used to have such lovely . . . lovely . . .'

'What do you think?'
She empties drawers full of soft bras and nighties
onto the floor.
Surrounded by debris.
Life at full tide
was just a big shopping trip.
'I've got nothing to wear,' she states
calmly surveying
a cupboard full of clothes.

Junk

Get rid of it all.
Make archaeologists accountable
for digging more of it up.
Old stuff.
Skeins and strands and tentacles,
browning indoor plants.
Bits and broken pieces,
Watches with inscriptions
that don't tock.
Knick-knacks.

Shoes full of smells.
Old hats, grim faces
old hates, odd glances.
Cracked handbags.
Bad dreams, forgotten pledges
mirrors with no frames,
might-have-beens.
Four potato peelers, rusty, from Taiwan.

Don't even give it away for a song.
Burn the St Vincent de Paul's.
Stand on a headland and fling it over the edge.
The ocean glitters
with family-crested silverplate.
Nests of occasional tables go in at a cant.
Bakelite radios that still play
surge in the waves.
'Thor' washing machines agitate, churning sand.
Bagfuls of family photos subside silently.

Robyn Archer

The Menstruation Blues

Chorus

I got the menstruation, the menstruation blues.
I got the menstruation, the menstruation blues.
And I got 'em so hard I don't know how to lose them.

I can feel my life blood flowin', flowin' down the drain
And the hardest damn thing to face is that next month it's all
   gonna happen again

I got a pain in my guts and my head is spinnin' around
I feel like the lowest kind of animal crawlin' on the ground

I can't chuck, I can't even fuck
Honey this thing has put me out of luck

No one wants to mouth around that fishy old smell
Lordy I'm so lonely and I feel like hell

I had to spend my dope money on a bunch of fanny rags
I'm 'bout to tell you this thing is gettin' to be a drag

Pamela Brown

Summer Icebox

those nights / summer / we sat
collating pornographic magazines
me stoned on snow
and wanting andy warhol,
you boozing and smiling
rolling your wonderful eyes;
pop culture children / summer
getting older all the time /
you telling me / your airbrushed eyes /
elvis presley regularly
injects silicone
into his tiny cheeks

in 'leave it to beaver'
the tv mom
pulls her cakes,
already frosted,
from her tv oven / in surry hills
disposable underwear
becomes a comment
on the transiency of shit stains;
and we are living in letratone,
lop-sided and lonesome

/ but most of all
i liked you
when you fell over
into bourbon and cement.
the dope turned to concrete
in my stomach /

we saw dennis hopper posing
for jim beam bourbon advertisements
in esquire magazine; probably
dangerous, health questionable.
myths questionable;
is leon russell a chauvinist?
does cilla black have a colostomy?

/ i fell in love. with you.
after you told me
you were once
a fourteen stone
teenage buttercup
stuck in the wildmouse
roller coaster carriage.
you had to go round twice
till they came
with crowbars and ropes.
you reduced to ten stone. /

those nights / summer / i sat
reduced. tightly locked
in a pharmaceutical icebox.

Shaky Days

There is
   far too much
   weather
and
   too many incidents
   to get on
     the nerves
and   the lounge room
   looks like
   Opera In The Park Indoors.
A few sheets
   fall off the stand,
we lose the pianist
   to the
   southerly winds
where
   the expedition ends
   without discoveries.
The only
   steady thing
   is the music,
listening to
   Beethoven
   played by
     Alfred Brendel
wearing,
     so I'm told,
band-aids on every finger.

Vicki Viidikas

Going Down. With no Permanence

    I'm finding it impossible to begin, as you've ended so little. Last night my heart was a cheap flag waving to the nearest mirror in sight. I couldn't believe anything, seeing you drive away into others' arms. I'm no sweet virgin sock-washer either. So it's a matter of priorities I guess, just who wants to gamble. Talk of loving when there is no goal. Of belief when there is no road. My shoes are off and I'm walking barefoot. Down a long avenue of arms and kisses like knots. I'm getting tired and angry and thinking hell, I'm no sock-washer but there must be some other venue. I say my heart's big enough, it is. Every time it's eaten and collapses like a cough.

Today I'm trying to be reasonable. You're having breakfast with her. And there's no wedding ring, baby, fidelity, photo. No day to week token of what we have, a visible future. Crazy thing, it's happening everywhere. You waft into my room bringing delicious words, eyes, every other love you're still attached to, claim.

'I want all love-rites simultaneously.'

'I don't want to negate anything.'

Yes I understand. Incredible egotist! that one cracked heart is your own, gyrating in its uncertainty. Adoration. Adulation. Your heart seeks to reflect itself. Narcissus in the bath. How many loves do you want? Are you never full, leaky bucket?

And now you turn to your sock-washer reasoning socks are better than none. So you're surrounded again. Pursued and claimed. A shroud of outrage going up. Thinking of numbers and lines. It sharpens your humour. While I love this one the others must love me too. I'll keep my heart spinning. You think you're responding, keeping all the doors open. Yes. Yes.

This is the road my bare feet touch. Going down. The avenue with few affirmatives. Going down. With no permanence. This is the alternative to restrictions. So we assume. Without end.

The Country as an Answer

Endlessly walking the green hills in wet agitated goloshes,
trees lean outwards . . . they are nothing but leaves,
beautiful, coloured, falling and dying. The hills rise up,
breasts faces hands, their silence is complete.

I sit down and mud falls from my boots.

Cows plod towards a creek.

Not a single person is visible as the landscape flows and
dips . . . invisible dyings . . . no answer but what it is.
I have come a thousand miles to be here.

Peace, they tell me, sending messages from the black city.
This is what peace is? No use for the earth but as a place
to lie down in . . . faceless bodiless . . . passive with
admiration? There is no love or hate here, the contrast is
so subtle.

I feel the mud in my hands, the wet bright grass.

I understand I am meaningless here, merely another presence
. . . the trees do not recognise me, the cows do not remember.

The landscape has absorbed me, giving nothing to be desired.

Susan Hampton

Stockton

So I moved in with Nana, learning to cook
Irish stews in a long narrow kitchen with a smelly
gas stove and cupboards full of dinner sets
brought home by the boys full of grog. Or Pappy,
even fuller . . . but now dead, and so I inherit
a bamboo fishing rod. The breakwater, the breakwater.
I beachcomb or light fires and wait for the tide;
Nana is a pirate with her eyepatch from the cataract op.
We joke like sisters, scoffing brown muscat
with her pensioner pals and talking about who's died.
About arthritis and rheumatism and bad eyes and swollen
legs from falls on footpaths bumped up by tree roots.
I fit in remarkably well, here. I like her friends:
I trim their horny toenails with my pocketknife,
and cut their soft white hair which floats down
between the planks in the back verandah. One day
we empty the kitchen cupboards and wash everything:
a gravy boat, a vegetable dish that belonged to Pappy's
mother; glass soup bowls from the war. A cheese dish,
cut-glass water jugs. I wash the glass on a photo of
Nana at twenty with waist-length thick black hair, and I
say to her, Violet Lillian Gertrude Murphy.
'That's me,' she says. I decide to grow my hair.

Ode to the Car Radio

My right eye leaking blood coming home
from Casualty, patched, pirate view, & changing gears
past Rooms to Let $12 p.w. beside Surry Hills Smash Repairs
& a beer gut emerging from a pub door at ten, well,
you can picture the general scene
& click! clear as glass, the flute opening
to Prokofiev's *Romeo and Juliet*, cool & sweet
as a parkful of wet trees. Or the time
when a Sutherland aria came blasting through
the stink of rubber at a stop light in Lidcombe,
the volume accidentally on full & I grinned,
mouthing at surprised traffic-jammed faces.
Stopped for a milkshake at the corner of Norton
& Marion Streets, watching clouds coast by
the asbestos-looking steeple of that church—
Pachelbel's *Canon* (I want it played at my funeral)
and the church sailed in towards the city, freed,
the fierce white clouds stayed still.

Diesel fumes from a 470 to Lilyfield spread upward
to Mahler being grandiose, & disappear past a balcony
where an old man (knees spread like a cellist)
reads a newspaper, bowing the strings with scrawny
sun-bitten arms. Oxy-gear lights a Brandenburg Concerto,
car brakes are violins, a jay-walker is moved on
by a French horn. Before too long,
a jack-hammer in Woolloomooloo sounds reasonable
with pizzicato in one ear. The green brush graffitist
writes FRASER IS THE HILTON BOMBER to a Haydn trumpet
& during the downpour after a southerly buster, Debussy
dances on factory rooftops & front lawns &
the whole of Sydney heaves & drifts as the radio
lets out its congruous, incongruous love.

Inside the Skyscrapers

You're in one, so am I
and between us are the little old buildings,
if not 'fusty', then something similar,
real grime, real air
        —in here it's rarefied, isn't it—

the views are something else. Today
the sky's overt with a sort of sailing boat
pleasure, and the cranes dangle their wires
and big hooks aimlessly, as if windswept.
　　　　This room's all greys
except for my shirt, liquid on my arm,
and bright dark red. The director of this group
has gone to find some circular instruction
and the men opposite me begin telling jokes about contests.
The one where a dare about eating a budgie
ended in the bird being eaten by the darer
as well—they cut it in half. They roar laughing,
heads bunched under the window which gives me a view
of your building. Its CALTEX sign. Who owns mine
I don't know, the forces of capital, I suppose.
　　　　All morning I've been reading Anna Kavan
Followed by glimpses of one and then of several
abandoned cages of a travelling circus, and the
stretched jaws and skeletal midriff of a starved tiger
fighting the bars of the cage, the landscape behind
rainswept, a road crammed with panic-stricken
refugees, vehicles stogged in mud, overflowing the
bounds of the road.
　　　　The joking here goes on, tales of beer and vomit
then chairs tilt back to the floor as the director returns,
arms full of amending legislation from Central Office.
I have a sudden memory of lunchtime, a Chinese girl
carrying tulips from Martin Place. What's happening
with you?

Jennifer Maiden

Space Invaders

Shaun knows you mustn't wait
too long behind the barrier.
You are a target anywhere.
You skip, you strike, you kill
bigger bastards and you score.
He steers his tick-shaped ship across
the black dog universe until
it hits a jet fleet like
a phalanx of fleas and implodes with

the wan beep of a dying
electroencardiograph. He leans
crosslegged in taut boredom,
and hits with sensuous disgust
the infinity of shit he's known
others he's known to need: the stuff
you smoke, the stuff you spend,
the stuff you eat, the stuff
you have to suck at school.
He knows it's not as fucked
as the pokies his parents pull
next door. No handfuls
of shit fall out. His
second ship survives.
He still needs to use his aim,
his hand, his sight.
In spring again he thinks he'll shoot
more wildcats and rabbits with his mate.
He'd like to join the Army soon.
He has a hunter's eye for parasites.

In the Gloaming

The door isn't locked. You walk
through the empty rooms and look for a person—
then for a sick one, then for a dead.
There is only no one home. You aren't relieved.
From the inside, you lock the door.
You shelter in life-surfaces. An electric fire, both
elements wink up slowly. The kettle shivers. You
wish it would whistle, but it cuts out, too
automatic. But the coffee's warm. You pour
the milk from stout safe glass so that the cream
is the first to fall. You use beige quartz sugar
to thicken your drink. You overfill the cup.
The biscuits aren't rich enough. You search out
cake. Only the icing is stale, and it will
turn tender with hot water in your mouth.
Corpse-air outside makes 'gloaming' tangible.
You shut it out. Venetians snap together.
You sit with your food and beverage until
the capillaries on your calves form a tartan:
red, blue, white, green from electric comfort.

You press your fingers into bruises.
Your shins ache with revival, bright as sex.
The heat in your ankles and throat are the same.
There are too many lights turned on
in the house and you love the guilt.
You are in a house alone and know it, for
you are not home. The furniture cannot
answer you here like dresses or duty.
You make your fingernails scrape white runs
down and up your arid legs. Your skin
has become the weather again. There is
no key in the door yet, no hope. Sweet coffee
thins within your thorax like a sun.

Turning the Bulls Around

               1991. For the first time,
this year at the Sydney Show, they
turned the bulls around. They
hadn't thought of it before. The bulls
had always been shown rump out:
                         the way
that they were herded in. The brown
and black tonweights would squat
on legs numbly folded, which later
carried them as tremblingly
again as poddy calves. It must
have been thought that lolling eye-
to-eye with the spectators would
alarm bulls, but they actually
seemed to like it, and some gave
wonderful testosterone shudders
and snorts and their fame-drunk gaze
suggested a chorus of 'My Way', like
Saddam at his birthday party. Some
blinked with Bush's hyperthyroid eyes.
                         I
have never really gone along
with the thought that things like wars
are caused by men not women. Still,
these creatures roared theatrically because
their breath left the blank wall.
                    And they stir,
and their vast, brute, tragic faces cry
and deepen when the stroking hand withdraws.

Vicki Raymond

Static

On a dry day, everything you touch
in the office gives you a shock:
pins, staples, the metal edge of a desk.
You can even feel it through your clothes,
which crackle lightly like tinfoil.
It's as though you were turning into
something not rich, but strange; your hair
floats out like Coleridge's
after he'd swallowed honeydew.
There's always someone playing Sistine God,
walking around looking for Adams of both sexes
to galvanize with a sharp finger.
You grow wary: you grasp handles,
like nettles, hard. It's the soft touch that hurts.

Laundromat

I glance from my book to see
a Bengali musical
flickering black and white.
A dimpled hero spins
like a load of washing
across the screen, singing.

The hero is suffering.
His brothers are plotting against him.
Even his mother has offered
the ultimate insult:
she has given him left-overs,
which he has eaten, not knowing.

His wife, who is loyal,
has found that out, and told him:
hence this aria.
Later, a smiling Krishna,
wreathed in flowers, appears
to vindicate and console.

The laundromat man says:
'This film is about Fate.
You know, Fate in God? It's meant
to make you think deeply about this.
What are you reading?' '*Ivanhoe*,' I say.
'That's good,' he says, 'Sir Walter Scott.'

An Episode of the Class Struggle

(A Brechtian interlude)

As Dives was stepping off the escalator
at Camden Town Station, he
was accosted by a pauper named Lazarus,
who asked him for the price of a cup of tea, tra la la la la.

'Regretfully,' replied Dives,
'I must refuse your request;
although your predicament is touching,
I am a Socialist, tra la la la la.

'And I believe that charity
would convey the false impression
that the rich are kind and generous,
and thereby delay the Revolution, tra la la la la.'

'What you say sounds very reasonable,'
said Lazarus, drawing his knife,
and, stabbing the plutocrat through the liver,
deprived him of money and life, tra la la la la.

Now Dives is sitting on brimstone
tormented by pitch-forking devils,
while Lazarus sits in a prison cell,
studying for his O-levels, tra la la la la.

Lazarus is studying Nietzsche,
for Marx only makes him yawn,
but Dives is at the North London Crematorium,
scattered all over the lawn, tra la la la la.

Open Day, Highgate Cemetery

From Waterlow Park, the slurred chromatics
of a brass band tuning up
float to the summer visitors.
Volunteers are clearing brambles
from the choked paths.
The claiming, exclaiming birds
sketch unseen boundaries.
High heels balance on cracked slabs;
Victorian inscriptions are read out.

Around the gate, we drink weak tea
from paper cups, accept a leaflet,
latch on to tours,
and tell each other it's not morbid.
'It's history,' we chirp, disclaiming
the act we all perform
at the door of one tall tomb:
on tiptoe, we peer through the grille,
and drop back, disappointed by darkness.

Chat Show

'You never married.' 'No,' he said,
'Relationships were not my *forte*.'
'Any regrets?' 'Ah . . .' Here we supply
the bitter-sweet accompaniment.
Of course. But he had higher ends
than procreation. Who could fill
the deep well of his genius? 'Perhaps.'

'You never married.' 'No,' she said,
'I wasn't asked.' Poor thing,
ceaselessly shovelling her work
into that lack. 'Regrets?'
'No, none at all.' Oh well, she would say that.

Night Piece (Freycinet Peninsula)

There is a parrot which has a cry
like a woman screaming.
This sound is disconcerting
when you first hear it,

but you get used to it.
The squabble of possums
over an apple core
will draw you from sleep

like a cork from a bottle,
but you get used to it.
On the other hand, our frogs
make a deep plunking sound

not unlike a guitar,
and the crickets here keep up
a shimmering vibrato
which children have mistaken

for the twinkling of stars,
and the trees shed their bark
all night with a stiff rustling.
Some things will always be strange.

Edith Speers

Confessional

In the car we face forward.
It's easier.
The road occupies your eyes
and mine can dwell on the landscape,
which reassures me—

that meat and milk still walk on four feet
and eat the grass that grows
in quadrilaterals defined by title deeds
and tautened wire;

that trees still infiltrate the earth
with sneaky fibres almost sentient
in their greed, and feed off the empty air
with flat busy fingers;

that houses still squat foursquare,
fat and sedentary with furniture,
and lap up a daily traffic of tricycles,
fly spray, freezer bags, and people;

that this rolling globe still trundles
mundanely along its way, while the galaxies
like free-spinning flywheels
hurtle unendingly nowhere.

And I accept it all.
It's perfectly convincing. So why
do I choke on a gnat, having swallowed a camel?
You tell me your intimate truths.

You produce the facts.
Each one is solid, polished, gratifying;
and you line them up like abacus beads
in rows of immaculate reasoning.

It's plain for any eyes to see that they can account
for everything. It all adds up,
you tell me, and what's more you believe it. So why
do I wonder why, and just exactly to whom
are you so busy lying?

Jean Kent

After Illness, Grace Notes

i   *Eyeing the Blade*

Because there is grace in small particulars

(the white eye of the sewing machine light
unwinking; its big mouth dripping
a thin thread of web;

these pieces of carved-out material
unexpectedly stable in my hand or
the turned-back petals of the hyacinth
shivering slightly on the table as the machine
lets its black belt fly and there is no judo mat
for the flower's startled perfume
to tumble onto—)

It is possible now
to take the green-handled scissors

It is possible to cut two curves
as touching as scallop shells:
a Peter Pan collar for a blouse.

Because this morning there was a red rainbow
with freak defiance climbing up
through smog and sun-nudged cloud
to a heaven too remote from the hard earth
of this world—it faded, dissolved when I looked

straight into it, but a minute later
when the eye was not quite on it,
gracefully, like a friend offering forgiveness
returned

It is possible
carefully, to do this

and also to take trouble
slicing into interfacing, knowing
as the white stiff stuff
lies thankless as bones

that there will be no nick
under the surface, no thought
of turning the scissor blade back
upon my own slack skin.

And because one chirpy silver-eye in spite
of the cat rolled up like a cannonball beneath
its sparkler-burst of cheeps still rocks
upon the long arcing arms of the delicately
new-leaved and furry-budded mulberry tree,

In spite of this lance of wind
which cuts like a death wish through the tight
balloons of light, falling at last,
shivering history, headfirst
into earth

It is possible now to want
to live

possibly today   that it will be enough
for those two collar pieces tacked at last
about the neck of the blouse
to be only themselves

and not what they lean towards
down the resigned slope of shoulder-blades:

such small, earthed wings.

ii   *No Don Quixote in Sight*

Now the violin, gliding like ink
over the etched copper plate of days
belonging to long dead Brahms
releases again a wet shining print

and hangs it from the ceiling.

A veil of hope, flimsy as light. But
give it time. It may yet drip sweet
and sleek with morning fragrance
as a just-washed sheet, pegged between
pawpaws and mulberry buds on the line.

Like a snail it may yet
hold air, unafraid.

So. I shall live a little longer.
I am prepared for it now
as this moment of radiant wood
plants a mast within the caught
breath of the room. The tight trunk creaks:

Pain blooms; fades.

With perfect chivalry through these spaces now
grace notes turn   settling in my hands
along lifelines as deep as the veins in leaves.
Silence lifts a corner of the print.
Seconds float up.

Through billowing sky   as if at windmills
the   slow   day   tilts

Clerical Assistant

In purple pedal pushers and cyclamen shoes
(with ankle bells),
she plonks behind her desk
like a cork, parted from Bodega.
Escaping every morning a Housing Commission flat,
why isn't she nineteen in Paris,
fizzy with adventure,
dizzy on one meal a day?
She starves instead, not-digesting papers
by forty-year-olds who say
(madeleining their Paris every Sunday
with croissants flaky from Balmain):
Study at Tech! Get your HSC!
Shivery before their sheltered sparks
she remembers her father
who dumped his family like tea-leaves—
and she studies the dates
till payday. Dreams, sometimes
of floating free—
renting a house near McDonalds.
She reads the *To Lets* when she's finished faking
her flexi-sheets . . . Purrs the phone
into old friends' ears: *Waddya reckon?*
But it never comes off.
The future flickers from her
as they rage all night at *Selinas* instead.
Mornings she lets her fingers travel
the typewriter. All through the pages
of *Future Options: A Workshop*
for Women Returning to the Workforce,
the forty-year-olds find her present
of white-out—blind gasps of blizzard breath
waiting to escape.

Ania Walwicz

The Abattoir

I owe my living to the abattoir. My father, the manager, sat in the office. Red brick, smelling of death. These dumb and frightened sheep that travelled at night. So I could eat them. Each stamp, clip in the office, smelled of slaughter. The purple, indelible pencil left a dot on the pink tongue tip. So very extra mauve like mark. Number or tattoo. Counted the stamp marks on the flesh pink, alive yesterday. And killed. These white paper sheets all written neatly and typed. These tiny pencil marks spelled the ending. The glazed, dumb eyes of the cows waiting. That I ate. That lived inside me. That I became. My vet dad, giving me needles. Like a pig. Earned money for my typewriter in the abattoir. Killing thousands of sheep and eating them all and every one. The blood seeping through the oil paper, these presents he got me. This meat. Red steaks I'd put in my hand. Lovely ladies, each one. Put my hand in the mince. Flesh squelching inside my fist. That's me. In here. Pink and gushing. One little scratch. And I'm one pig. Pigs at the cattle market. Pinks in the abattoir. My father, the artificial inseminator of cows, sits at his desk and kills. With his purple pencil. These healthy butchers. Very happy. Slicing away. Their stomachs taut. Looked at them, excited with their knives. The butcher at home, bending wire in his singlet. I had a cook. Had cooks. Never had the butcher. This butcher cut a piece. Put red meat in his raw mouth. My father stood next to the cow. The pig squealed. The healthy, young, beautiful butchers sang in their silver room. Hosed the floor. Sunshine in their mirrors. Lights in their glass. Glistening pink flesh on their plate. Sausages in my hand. Warm butcher's hands on my breasts.

The Fountain

I saw a fountain. One night. Big golden . With yellow lights shining. One fountain. Moth drawn to it. I cross the street. I'm looking. The centre golden fountain. Water flying. The jet shooting up. All lit up. My fountain. My heart beating. Fast. I saw this fountain. Gold light in the centre of the park . My fountain. All lit. My fountain. Showing off. I was a fountain. All lit. My heart red as my lips. I was looking at the fountain go up. I was gushing looking. I was the fountain. I was the fountain in the middle of the park. I was all lit at night. I was the centre of the park in the darkness. I was gold water.

I was the fountain. I was so young. I was night walking . I was watching myself be. I was golden shooting. I was seeing myself get so up. I was the fountain . I was gushing. I was excited with myself. Shooting golden. I was all in. I was the centre of the pin point. I was a fountain. I was the beautiful splashing, rushing, jumpy, all wet fountain. I was all lit up. And up. I was a fountain. I was the fountain right in the middle. I didn't need anybody else. I was in true true love with myself. I was the fountain. I was golden up flying water. With my light reflector. With my up movement. I was the water rocket. All flying up. I was only looking. I just wanted myself. I was the fountain.

Judy Small

From the Lambing to the Wool

My father was a cocky as his father was before him
And I married me a cocky nearly fifty years ago
And I've lived here on this station and I've seen the seasons
    changing
From the drought round to the flooding, from the lambing to the
    wool

Chorus

And there've been times when I've wondered if it all was worth
    the doing
And there've been times when I've thought this was the finest
    place there is
For though the life here's never easy and the hours are long and
    heavy
I'm quite contented nowadays to have joined my life to his

Together through the '30s while others' lives were broken
We worked from dawn to twilight to hold on to what was ours
And at night we'd sit exhausted and I'd stroke his dusty forehead
With him too tired to talk to me and me too tired to care

CHORUS

And the children came unbidden bringing laughter to the
    homestead
And I thanked the Lord my sons were young, too young for battle
    then

And I counted myself lucky to lose no-one close to family
Though the neighbours lost their only son, sold up and moved
    to town

CHORUS

And the children have grown and left me for careers in town and
    city
And I'm proud of them, but sadly, for none chose station life
And now I smile to hear them talking of the hard slog in the office
For when I think of working hard I see a cocky and his wife

CHORUS

Mothers, Daughters, Wives

Chorus

The first time it was fathers
The last time it was sons
And in between, your husbands marched away with drums and
    guns
And you never thought to question
You just went on with your lives
'Cause all they taught you who to be was mothers, daughters,
    wives

You can only just remember the tears your mothers shed
As they sat and read their papers through the lists and lists of dead
And the gold frames held the photographs that mothers kissed each
    night
And the door frames held the shocked and silent strangers from
    the fight

CHORUS

It was twenty-one years later, with children of your own
The trumpet sounded once again, and the soldier boys were gone
And you drove their trucks and made their guns and tended to
    their wounds
And at night you kissed their photographs and prayed for safe
    returns
And after it was over, you had to learn again
To be just wives and mothers, when you'd done the work of men

So you worked to help the needy, and you never trod on toes
And the photos on the pianos struck a happy family pose

CHORUS

Then your daughters grew to women, and your little boys to men
And you prayed that you were dreaming when the call-up came
  again
But you proudly smiled and held your tears as they bravely waved
  goodbye
And the photos on the mantelpieces always made you cry
And now you're getting older and in time the photos fade
And in widowhood you sit back and reflect on the parade
Of the passing of your memories as your daughters change their
  lives
Seeing more to our existence than just mothers, daughters, wives

CHORUS

And you believed them

Dorothy Porter

*Wunjo**

Tonight
    my room is different,
        miraculous
I leave it
come back to it,
you're still in my bed—

you're smoking
you're propped up on my pillows
your naked skin pale   dark lovely
    in the light
        of my rickety reading lamp—

what have you looked at
    while I've been gone?
my shelves of books, my messy desk
    my glass of water . . .

*The rune of joy

P.M.T.

The moon is out this morning.
Full,
    and the yellow
      of old dentures.
Nothing like a moon
    in a fastidious T'ang poem
it stares through
    the mist, the traffic, my windscreen,
like a mesmerising chilblain.

The radio is a box of 'Fantales';
    gossip, rubbish
      and caramel.
I chew on it
thinking about
    my long weekend
      my lover's delectable mouth.
But the moonlight
    splashes on my driving hands
      like freezing water
and I count my jerky heart-beats
      backwards.

Nefertiti Rides Me

Nefertiti rides me.

Her cunt
    slippery on
      the hot skin
        of my belly.

She's sticky
with my glue—
    that high stink
      of seed!

My tongue
    tastes her sap
      a sweat-honey
        shot with salt

still wild
   in the corners of my
      mouth.

I want to hold her
I want to lie still
but she's not finished
   her eyes are shut
   her breath
     a stammering breeze
now, now
   oh, yes

she growls like the desert
   melts like sleep
     and annoints me
       exquisitely.

I'm her war horse
she looks down
   from hooded eyes
and laughs, laughs.

I love her more than Aten.

From *The Monkey's Mask*

Money for Nothing

'Lou, I feel like I'm talking
to a bunch of accountants

they keep asking
is there much money
in my line of work

I'm learning a lot
from these poets—
computers and tax evasion.'

'It's a grabby, grotty world
not much to go around.
Blame patronage, Jill,
grants, fellowships,
Writers-in-Residence
all that crap . . .

the kids go in
bright-eyed and bushy-tailed
the girls think they're Plath
without the loony bin
the boys wanna be discontinuous heroes
like a good-on-ya mate version
of Carver or Ondaatje

then the little buggers
have to watch
the smart old frauds
and smart young crawlers
split the spoils

and where's the poem in this?
they ask the dole
the dirty flat
and the genital warts

their zingy lives
blow out
while the deadshits
with the contacts
and gift of post-modernist gab
grab what's going.'

'What about you, Lou?'

'I've done the seventies trip, Jill,
I lived with an ideologically
small publisher
who couldn't flog a book
to her own mother

the pub readings
where you were lucky
to get a free beer

I reckon it's my turn
*money for nothing
and my chicks for free.*'

How Poems Start

Is this how poems start?

when every riff on the radio
hooks in your throat

is this how poems start?

when the vein under her skin
hooks in your throat

is this how poems start?

when insomnia pounds
like spooked black horses

when the day breaks
like car crash glass

tell me, Mickey,
you knew

tell me

does a poem start
with a hook in the throat?

Deb Westbury

Self Portrait in a Mirror

There's a triangular green smudge
on my self portrait.
It's only a profile and some hair
crouching beside a mirrored wardrobe.
So no one could tell it was me
pregnant and alone
in that old house at Shellharbour,
talking on the phone.

I worried on and off
about that oily smudge
on the subtle grey drawing.
I considered camouflage and solvents
but in the end I left it there,
a sacred symbol in a secret picture,
to remind me of the day
the portrait was complete,

The day I stood on my toes
and felt for it
amongst the relics and rubbish
on top of the wardrobe.
As I pulled it free
the darkness rained
coloured crayons.

Green struck the portrait
as it fell
noisily
in the sleep-quiet room,
the only room I'd ever painted.
It was yellow
because I wished my son
a world of light.
Wisteria crowded purple at the window.
Accidents happen.

Albatross Road

Since the big trees were all taken
you can see into the colourless scrub
through a scattering of skinny saplings
where black men gather in the shadows
smoking and drinking
to remember with these rites
their mute women
their brothers in lock-ups
their children in white schools.
Smoke and murmurs
rise from the sunless clearing
where they sit on burnt-out logs
watching the road.

Young sailors
speed down this road from base
to town
and back again
raw country boys drunk
and sweaty with the mystery of their bodies
in uniform
and the power
of their machines
so ready in this rushing of blood
to forget, to kill, to die.
The navy has erected
a sign
that keeps a toll
of those injured and killed here
and reminds them that their families
and the navy
need them.

Waiting for the bus,
Koori girls bloom like hibiscus
on the dusty shoulders
of the road out of town.

Judith Beveridge

Fox in a Tree Stump

I gripped the branch
and waited in a paddock that ran on
over harder and harder earth.
Leaving me with smoke and the stick
to beat the fox, my uncle drove off.

Terror barrel-rode through my stomach.
I knew my uncle's quick rabbit-skinning hands,
his arms like dry river-beds dammed at the shoulders,
his voice harsh, kelpie-cursing
would not understand if I let the fox run to the bush.

Fox-hairs of dust sweated in my palms.
I stood in the exhaust of leaves
the short time it takes a tongue
to reach into a hurting body and strike ashes.

A twig snapped. The fox stood, coughing.
The branch on its neck
rang like a shot:
a shot so loud it shook out a flock
of galahs from their trees,
cracked like a wave
the buried sleep of rabbits.

When my uncle came back, he threw
the charred body into a ditch.
I turned away kicking earth over the bloodspots of fire
and prayed not to waken
another animal from the wheat.
I was nine years old. All my life
I'd stuck close to my yelled name.

I was a child praying for the dark
each time the sun caught my uncle's eye.

The Lyre Birds

Somewhere in the bush, hiding as long as they can,
domestic as soil, they scrape the hard earth
with their feet, making serious men-at-work sounds—
or pretending in their voices to be other than themselves.

These birds, from old-country Australia,
when everything was bush-fire charcoal, scrub.
Shy of their own language,
they exist still in their wingless rituals

amongst the bush-vowels of the parrots,
the mynas, the Dubbo-voiced galahs.
They can imitate any sky, any tree, bird by bird; make
a branch crack with fire in a whip-bird's throat.

Not much to see: tail like brown bracken and built
for miles and miles of the same scrub.
You can hear them call to each other
with a whole country's voice: pinehigh whispers,

water falling, a magpie's swagman whistle,
the downpour of wings, twitterings
from the long coops of grasses and they can steal
the wind's voice: a stockwhip at their throats; or repeat

note by industrial note the timber-mills, chain-saws . . .
But I imagine them long ago, when all was bush—
at dusk, wandering in pairs—
relaxed peacocks among the old gums;

they believed they were the feathered men
who danced the corroborees.
Now, scavengers of sound, like migrants
they've learned to live off foreign sounds in a new country,

to repeat another country's parrot culture,
to keep anonymous, alive.
But sometimes they forget and call to each other
in their own tongue, remembering a time

when ring after ring of men stopped,
got up, stomped the ground, danced, stomped again
danced and sang their own voices back to them.

Hannibal on the Alps

Tonight, it's quiet. Exhausted my men sleep
though they've learned to waken
from their best dreams. Our weapons
at least temper sleep like whores.

Below the small campfires burn out.
I can remember our farewell fires
on the plains of Utica and on the harbours
as our sails tusked the wind to Spain.

Perhaps we should have taken the sea—
the Mediterranean soft under our backs.
Here, the wind's cold and smells of wolves
I've seen rip our young elephants

like soft rind. And even now I hear
those terrified cries of my men and my battle
elephants that stumbled the precipice.
Nights pass, but time's no champion.

Tonight, the cold sacks my sleep.
If only I could be one of my deserters
asleep under the glossy stars, or by now
drunk on the musty grape of Andalusia

clamouring for music and extravagance.
Now, I listen as the wolves
drive a goat off into the valley.
At dawn we count our losses and move south.

Gig Ryan

Not Like a Wife

He questions her, his face soft with lovely money.
Be my mistress. He's French, polite as corruption.
Yes. Her clothes are dirty. Love has made me poor.
She leans against the flimsy cupboard, wrapping her face up
in her hands. I loved a rich man
once, but I was never blonde, and suntans you know,
so bland. I never looked American enough
on the beach.

I'll take you to Bangkok he says, the jewellery.
I can't wear it. The nightclubs. Yes.
You could look like a million dollars you know,
touching her shirt collar, if you had it.
I can't cook. His dark eyes soft and persistent
as flesh, wise with money he talks.
You like it here yes, you find character in poverty?
His arms snatch the whole creaking house up.
He's laughing at the plaster. You're so frank and evasive.
It's alright, really, tense as a movie,
watching carlights flash above the bed.
He loved me once. You're new, aren't you.

The sink's blocked in Darlinghurst.
I never could eat spaghetti effectively,
too unmarried or something.

If I Had a Gun

I'd shoot the man who pulled up slowly in his hot car this
                                            morning
I'd shoot the man who whistled from his balcony
I'd shoot the man with things dangling over his creepy chest
in the park when I was contemplating the universe

I'd shoot the man who can't look me in the eye
who stares at my boobs when we're talking
who rips me off in the milk-bar and smiles his wet purple smile
who comments on my clothes. I'm not a fucking painting
that needs to be told what it looks like.
who tells me where to put my hands, who wrenches me into
                                          position
like a meccano-set, who drags you round like a war
I'd shoot the man who couldn't live without me
I'd shoot the man who thinks it's his turn to be pretty
flashing his skin passively like something I've got
to step into, the man who says *John's a chemistry Phd
and an ace cricketer, Jane's got rotten legs*
who thinks I'm wearing perfume for him
who says *Baby you can really drive* like it's so complicated,
male, his fucking highway, who says *ah but you're like that*
and pats you on the head, who kisses you at the party because
everybody does it, who shoves it up like a nail
I'd shoot the man who can't look after himself
who comes to me for wisdom
who's witty with his mates about heavy things
that wouldn't interest you, who keeps a little time
to be human and tells me, female, his ridiculous
private thoughts. Who sits up in his moderate bed
and says *Was that good* like a menu
who hangs onto you sloppy and thick as a carpet
I'd shoot the man last night who said *Smile honey
don't look so glum* with money swearing from his jacket
and a 3-course meal he prods lazily
who tells me his problems: his girlfriend, his mother,
his wife, his daughter, his sister, his lover
because women will listen to that sort of rubbish
Women are full of compassion and have soft soggy hearts
you can throw up in and no-one'll notice
and they won't complain. I'd shoot the man
who thinks he can look like an excavation-site
but you can't, who thinks what you look like's for him
to appraise, to sit back, to talk his intelligent way.
I've got eyes in my fucking head, who thinks if he's smart
he'll get it in. I'd shoot the man who said
Andrew's dedicated and works hard, Julia's ruthlessly ambitious
who says *I'll introduce you to the ones who know*
with their inert alcoholic eyes
that'll get by, sad, savage, and civilised
who say *you can* like there's a law against it

I'd shoot the man who goes stupid
in his puny abstract how-could-I-refuse-she-needed-me
taking her tatty head in his neutral arms like a pope
I'd shoot the man who pulled up at the lights
who rolled his face articulate as an asylum
and revved the engine, who says *you're paranoid*
with his educated born-to-it calm
who's standing there wasted as a rifle
and explains the world to me. I'd shoot the man who says
Relax honey come and kiss my valium-mouth blue.

Let's Get Metaphysical

It's party-time in Darlinghurst, but he's sick of hairstyles
and those oracles of fun you give away like nuts.
Here it's raining in the kitchen, his black eyes glimpse
                                        virtue.
We hide friends under the bed
and can't get out of the room, stifling and affectionate.
How can you dance with your sprained ankle?
But you can't step back and separate the object from the
                                        process.
This thing is beyond love, beyond the brain's split.
The walls are singing with blue love
and the yellow sky dances with me
on days like this.

Enlightenment can't last, its silent smiling adventure.
I thought there was more to you.
The telephone is hot metaphysically
but his material presence is the limit.
What are you doing for lunch? I'm starting a charity until it
                                        stops
or else I'm giving it to you. The city like a map
isn't spontaneous. Listen to the lift's electric bell
as people freely pour out, and your free hour
wriggles to the window and jumps.
I don't like it when his body talks.

Disinformation

1

The fireworks of peace and celebration go up in the harbour
above the warships. Sailors strut through town
adored by skint women who, for a job, will cheer their garish
flag
One's trippy and bursts into the flat
jawing the air with a knife
He was disinformed. The pictures, the hype
that rev a plane across the Gulf of Sidra
mill in his baseball head until Intelligence chucks him

2

Our clown Prime Minister jostles on the steps,
unable to dissemble,
unable to not be loved by Indonesia, France, Chile, China
He troths the Bases, not alienated anymore
He clucks his timely personality
The sin of doubt assails the booths
He holds his broken minister in a camera grip
and weeps a tub
'Your women are beautiful,' says the Yank
in relay with his Navy darkening the harbour

Poem

The day is beautiful
He doesn't love me
Pieces of me fly in formation
across the sky's blue lung
Clouds of white hope
the beautiful afternoon
drifts like childhood
The green and yellow trees
fountain over you
Vines of memory
your rubbed face
Cars come home from work
The day is beautiful
its white christening shawl
its winding cloth

Sarah Day

Table Laid for One

He goes home to her each day for lunch
and sits alone
trickling spoonfuls of salt
from imitation crystal.
Lunchtime. The sweetness of baked pumpkin
mingles with the acrid air
of beans whose green seeps
through perforations in the pot-divider;
mingling also with memories
of schoolday noons,
grey shorts flapping about pale knees,
a cap that shadowed spacious brow
and small features.
The fact that nothing's changed
(except the taunting hurt of walking home)
is unnoticed. Piling, falling,
salt slides down the even pyramid.
He touches the picalilli
with his finger,
tests it
with a tentative untasting tongue.
Next door she warms the aluminium teapot
waiting for the kettle on the stove.
A speck of lamb fat
stings the loose flesh on her arm,
she rubs it absent-mindedly
with thick old palm.
When he finishes,
she presents the milk pudding,
sets it on the half-clothed table.
Later she sees him to the door,
watches while the well-preserved sedan
backs slowly down the drive.
Her hand half raised
he does not turn.
'How like his father.'
The frosted door latches,
she shuffles back
into the darkened dining room,
pauses to catch her breath
against his tall chair.

The smooth-skinned surface
of the untouched pink
inside the glass bowl
trembles slightly and is still.

Kissing the Bubble

This girl next to me begins to scream.
I hit her. There is not enough space
for so much scream. We have to stay calm
I try to explain and she stops but
we are all hemmed in still
by that great foam rubber scream of hers.
The light, I nearly said *cabin light*
because there is something about this
which is like flying in an aeroplane at night,
is on. Hoo-ray General Motors electricals
I'll drop a sincere line of felicitation
when I get out of here. Yep, light's still on,
there are my old bulwark mates in the front seat,
here's this girl whose name I do not know,
owner of the scream, with my arm about her;
radio's playing, Seppelt Rhine Riesling
comfortable between my thighs; scenario
basically as it was five minutes ago, forty feet up
on dry dock before Victor thought he'd impress us
with the V8's reverse acceleration
and got it wrong, the tilt, glide and slow bump
like lunar landing looks on TV. Four wheels stable
on the sea bed and it's time for a snort I say
just to calm the nerves because when we open
those windows we're going to need to be cool
as proverbial cucumbers. That water is going to
hit us like . . . Like Blazes, thought I'd lost
my head off my neck for a jiff and here's my arm
around Whatsername's knees and her shoe in my mouth
and my mates up front going like blinking
dirty clothes in a washing machine.
Just wait a sec, I say to myself,
this is all going to equalise soon and
thank Christ for the aerodynamic-super-funky-
sling-back that's crooning this bubble
and we dip can dip like goldfish kissing pure air;

Heaven but it can't last, so it's out with
Big Harry first 'cause he's going to need
a push from behind—the rest of us
pop like corks, too many feet more and we'd have
sunk like stones before these glorious stars
were twinkling in our eyes.
Shredding our fingers and toes on barnacles
and this dickhead flies over in Y-fronts
like Icarus, his badge winking up above
from a neatly folded uniform—
would've bloody drowned if we hadn't hauled him out
and what does he say first if it isn't
'nominate us for the George mate,'
us like a row of bloody shags on a rock.

Plenary

You arrive without knocking
and I am looking without warning
at your ankles and sandshoes
just when I have become cow
and the grass on the high hills
tears in my teeth with a sound
of breaking porcelain;
heads stoop around me,
black and white right-angles;
I am gazing down the straight seam
of my spine across a horizontal mirror
to ellipses of blackwood,
reverse shadows in heavy silhouette
on the paddock, random as patches
on the herd's back. If sky were
emerald, clouds black as cows
then the whole might be a variation
on the same theme and we might be
tree, cloud, animal, shadow.
•
A while ago, wind blew through my branches,
wood sprouted from pelvis into tree-limb,
sap rose to the tide of a silent sea
and water seeped through clay
to hair-fine roots; wood from trunk up,
earth from groin down. The two legs
white as tooth root, are gone;

gone too, the slit-in-the-middle receptor,
giver, lover, lover's mouth.
Far, far from the sensual single-tailed mermaid.
Below this waist, there is only net skirt
through which waves draw and breathe.
I am water. I am clay.
Winds sway me from the waist,
play my arms like pianos, like chimes
like seaweed in a current. This is like
water this wind. It is kind
and terrible. The will cries out
in the sweeping.

Dipti Saravanamuttu

Sealing the Deal

How to recall the precise shape of a person.
Or rather, the shape they created in our minds.
Before, during and after another lunatic conversation
With the generosity of the truly broke
forgiving the truly vicious,
doubled over in a phone-box
to be reminded of the generally discrete
charm of the bourgeoisie—

his cryptic Superman, he agrees
complicated lovers are like ocean views,
addictive, and far too salty.
I wish him a brace of credit cards
Many Overseas Holidays,
unlimited elegance, his own
strategic international fuck-list
and similar things that should
just make him laugh. And to know
that it's *all* play-art, and needn't
be otherwise. Still,
there's something about being back
in neat Keating's Australia.
The clichés come true,
like the light, the sense of space
making coming home like driving
from the inner-city to Coogee
writ large;

the feeling of a horizon
being just down the street/
across the water and
on days you feel like smiling,
in everybody's eyes.

Like Yeast in Bread

In the old women's ward
at Neringah hospital
an Ukrainian grandmother is requested
to sing a song. She replies:
'In Ukrainian, songs are dreams.'
Awake to death, my grandmother
has asked for someone to stay back, each night.
It is the year of Halley's comet.
My grandmother, who may be in her nineties
does not know her age.

My aunts have come from England.
A responsible twenty-five-year-old, I stay
my turn overnight, every fourth night,
in the milky blue light
of the night ward, where noise
feels like a hard object
dropped into stillness like glass.

Of her, I have a lifetime
of too few memories.
Unlike anyone we ever love
she'd never hurt me, giving
serenity rather than contradiction.
'We don't love people because
they are clear water,' she chided gently
once, after she'd observed
a familiar clash of temperament.

My mother's mother kicks the hospital sheets
and asks if the sound
of the air-conditioner is a river.
'Mehe gungak lungethe?'
The spirit of place
sits waiting for me all day
in the garden, while she sleeps
clutching the reflection of her hand.

Hers will be the first death
in the new land.
Before any birth or marriage,
this grief empties me like shock.
Back in Maroubra I stroll around
feelingless, like a mask that
has to absorb whatever image comes next—
her raucous laughter,
her mobile face and hands.

I walk through the shopping mall
beside the sea, trying to write
an elegy in all or any appropriate form:
like strokes painted by a fool or madwoman
because she needed art, and suddenly
a nine-year-old Vietnamese boy
in the Christmas show is singing
'I love Aeroplane Jelly . . .'
in an incredibly high octave
before a beaming, bemused audience.

Alison Croggon

Songs of a Quiet Woman

lurching delicate as a snow queen down this street of greys
unfocussed exactly enough to miss the businessman
goggling at my stockings   deciding
(as I twitch primly into my tram seat   my handbag
nestled on my lap like a puppy)   deciding
this will be a day of minor survivals:
etching a bloody mouth in fluorescent mirrors
or idly lacquering a hand of claws:
small weapons for a small war
•

there is one streetlight which always
blinks off whenever I walk near it
come home late and secretarial
to the hint of cats and cooking—
silently inside me something flexes
something unsurprised

men of course   lately they are kind to me
although an acid starting in my sweat
erodes me like an argument:
snatched by hesitation in a shop
eloquent and secret with the smell of him
I feel sureness swelling like a bruise
forcing blood into lips   breathless and reverent
this pearl in the corruption of my belief

•

(yes please no trouble thankyou mother
it's been a pleasure because I do not know
how to be angry or ugly mother—
granny addled with sherry under bombs
in Winchester never raised her voice
or said a word back to your father
no matter what women or what insults:
her eighty year old skin is white and powdered
and now she pisses in the basin mother
and I know the proper way to lay tables)

•

to other things I turn the eye of god.
the tv's gorgon eye has glazed me over
and nothing touches me at all:
not famine fire fear or revolution.
only a twitching child in Beirut
firmly stroked to stillness by a nun:
he stared at her with eyes as black as hunger.
I wept then for the simple magic of hands

•

the routine of coffee   the complicity
of cigarettes and gossip
this gentle leaning over narrow tables
into the sly glass of recognition:
I know I am dishonest in my dress
(she says to me)   I know I am dishonest
but all I ever knew was how to lie

Lindy

at the end of a panic of voices
strangely the camp stilled
its secret tented passions
hearing the morning bruise

with a thousand spiteful letters
days and days of locked rooms:
indifferent in the breaking light
the rock said nothing

there were others   there were always others
dogs running in the hungry twilight
she was alone only at the crisis
when she screamed the world bent its greedy ear
when she smiled photographers came to listen
her face hooded itself and slept
in a chrysalis of stone

the icons of her dreams scattered in the desert
slowly they gathered them   dog's tooth   torn cloth
and labelled them with the ardour of converts:
she reassembled her voices in the silence
the crow sat in her larynx telling the same truth always
the oracle broke and bled   the people turned away, debating
fashioning another legend

Charmaine Papertalk-Green

Wanna be White

My man took off yesterday
with a waagin*
He left me and the kids
to be something in this world
said he sick of being
black, poor and laughed at
Said he wanted to be white
have better clothes, a flash car
and eat fancy
He said me and the kids
would give him a bad name
because we are black too
So he left with a waagin.

*Waagin: East Coast word for 'white woman',
derived from 'white gin'.

Tracy Ryan

Killing Delilah

Because I have lived too long with her
and for her, blinding myself
by degrees, calling it love.
My other half, I said.
She became my interpreter.
I relied on her charms to get me through
a foreign land.
Strength was all I had
but she did away with it
quietly, while I slept
a lifetime
till her words spoke for me
and her ways won out.
I thought her face was my own face,
put faith in her social graces—
she was always in demand.
But sooner or later someone
was bound to ask for me.
Now is the moment of release,
my only chance.
My fingers are feeling for the cracks.
One sure blow is all it takes
to bring this house down.

City Girl

had a lover once who
always talked of the Blue
Mountains where
mauve light charms rifts
into gullies and poems
grow in lichen.

They met in town
down the alleys of Northbridge
one hour a week in his offices.
He regretted this tawdriness
unfortunate backdrop

to modern romance
somehow wrote sonnets to the highrise blocks—
all so much raw material.

His words made a way to
another world, pure pastoral
come live with me I'll leave my wife.

Try as she might she still saw
straight streets   slums   department stores
the soon-dead novelty of elsewhere;
herself in an old role
written out   discarded
said no and left
him momentarily at a loss
for metaphor.

Jemal Sharah

Black Swans in St James's Park

And so they have come to this:
a neglected pool,
paths snowflaked with spit
and—pellets enclosed in ice—
with green goose shit,
and a sky that seems as close as a coffin lid.

They will not bob again under a sky
of violent blueness, or feel the daylight crash
across them like a wave; only this trickle
of fatty sunshine will illumine their days.

Poor exiles.
But they are locals now—
in black winter street-clothes, they sift anxiously
among the plastic bags that clog the lake.

Pastoral

We have crossed over the stile, and entered
    this diffident landscape
we saw from the path, as if painted
    as neat as a book-plate.

The oat-grass, blown into plump sheaves,
    shines rust, silver and straw;
the verdigris blades of gum leaves
    are antiques from old wars.

Let us leave at the fence love and death,
    those great human themes:
look where a gum against copper earth
    like Kali dances and dreams.

Back at home there is radiant wood
    poised to fall into snow,
and apples, cheeks dawn-cold and red,
    clustering on the bough;

but we step through the wilderness now
    in an austere country:
we have left at the gate all we've learned
    and shall tread lightly.

Notes on Contributors

Susan Afterman (1947–) has also published poetry as Susan Whiting. Since the late 1980s she has lived in Israel and some of her longer poetry pursues Jewish themes.

Ethel Anderson (1883–1958) was born in England and educated in Sydney. After living in England and India, she returned to Australia in 1926 with her British army husband, who became aide de camp to the governor-general. Her collection of short stories, *At Parramatta* (1956), is her best-known work.

Robyn Archer (1948–) is well known as a cabaret singer, actress, writer and theatre director. She suggests that 'The Menstruation Blues' is the kind of song that should acquire new verses as years pass.

Dorothy Auchterlonie (1915–1991) was admired as the passionate literary critic, Dorothy Green, who wrote on Henry Handel Richardson and a range of literary and moral issues. She published only two books of poetry, *The Kaleidoscope* (1940) and *The Dolphin* (1967).

'Australie' (Emily Manning) (1845–1877), the first Australian-born woman poet of any standing, worked for a time as a journalist for the *Illustrated Sydney News* and the *Sydney Mail* in the 1850s.

Judith Beveridge (1956–) won the Mary Gilmore Award for her first book of poetry, *The Domesticity of Giraffes*, in 1988.

Lily Brett (1946–) was born in Germany and came to Melbourne with her parents soon after. She has published several books of poetry on Holocaust themes, and *The Auschwitz Poems* won the 1987 Victorian Premier's Award for Poetry. She moved to New York in 1990, and her latest book is a comic novel about New York Jews called *Just Like That*.

Pamela Brown (1948–) was one of the women who emerged among the experimental poets in Sydney in the early 1970s. She sees her poetry as interrelated with her work as artist, filmmaker, teacher, printer and publisher.

Joanne Burns (1945–) began performing and publishing poetry with poets such as Pamela Brown in Sydney in the early 1970s. Her readings have a reputation for liveliness and humour.

Caroline Caddy (1944–) lives in Western Australia. She has been publishing poetry since 1980.

Ada Cambridge (1844–1926) came to Victoria from England with her clergyman husband in 1870. More famous as a novelist than a poet, her fiction includes *A Marked Man, Materfamilias* and *The Three Miss Kings*.

Caroline Carleton (1820-1874), an Adelaide resident, won the Gawler prize in 1858 for her 'Song of Australia', which was set to music and was a contender for national song until the better-known 'Advance Australia Fair' was selected in the early 1980s.

Lee Cataldi (1942–) was part of the Sydney poetry scene in the 1970s, but since the mid-1980s has been teaching with the Warlpiri people in the Northern Territory.

Nancy Cato (1917–) was influenced by the Jindyworobak movement in Adelaide in the 1940s and 1950s. She has had great popular success with the re-publication of her novel about life on the Murray River, *All the Rivers Run.*

Alison Clark (1945–) lives in Sydney. Her second book of poems, *About Desire*, will be published soon.

Elsie Cole (*b*. 1892) lived in Melbourne and published at least two books of poetry in the 1920s.

Alison Croggon (1962–) came to Melbourne from South Africa. She won the Mary Gilmore award in 1992 for *This is the Stone*, and is known for her theatre reviews.

Zora Cross (1890–1964), an actress and journalist, became notorious in the 1910s and 1920s because of her candid poetry and her de facto relationship with David McKee Wright. The 'Vision' group, which included Jack Lindsay and Kenneth Slessor, mocked her mercilessly — possibly because she defied their masculinist ideals.

Sarah Day (1958–) teaches in Hobart and has published several books of poetry. Her first book of poetry won the Anne Elder award in 1987.

Dulcie Deamer (1890–1972) left New Zealand as a dancer, and was a leading figure in the bohemian set of Sydney during the 1920s. She liked to wear a leopard skin to fancy-dress parties.

Margaret Diesendorf (1912–1993) came to Australia from Vienna in 1939. A gifted linguist, she published several books of poetry in English, worked on *Poetry Australia*, and was active in the Sydney literary scene.

Rosemary Dobson (1920–) worked as an Angus & Robertson editor with Nancy Keesing, Douglas Stewart and Nan McDonald. Her training in the visual arts is obvious in much of her poetry, and she has established a reputation as one of Australia's foremost poets.

Dorothy Drain (1909–) wrote a weekly column for the *Australian Women's Weekly* from 1944 to 1972. Though a working journalist with other assignments, she managed to include a verse each week.

Eliza Hamilton Dunlop (1796–1880) was born in Ireland and came to Australia in 1838 with her husband, a police magistrate and protector of Aborigines in the Hunter Valley area of New South Wales. She was one of the first poets to attempt to transliterate Aboriginal songs and several of her poems were set to music by Isaac Nathan.

Anne Elder (1918–1976) danced (as Anne Mackintosh) in the Borovansky Ballet in her youth. Her second book of poetry, *Crazy Woman and Other Poems*, was published posthumously in 1977, and the Victorian Fellowship of Australian Writers administers the trust fund that awards a prize for poetry in her name.

Diane Fahey (1945–) lives in Adelaide and has published several books of poetry. Her poems won the Mattara Prize in 1985.

Mary Finnin (1906–) published most of her poetry in the 1930s, 1940s and 1950s. Her later work has religious themes.

Mary Hannay Foott (1846–1918) came to Melbourne from Glasgow as a child. She attended art school, became a teacher, and, following her marriage, a pioneer in south west Queensland. After the death of her husband, she became a journalist and literary editor for Brisbane journals. 'Where the Pelican Builds' was one of the most popular ballads of the turn of the century.

Mabel Forrest (1872–1935) worked as a journalist in Queensland. As well as four books of poetry, she published many romance novels, including *The Wild Moth* and *Hibiscus Heart*. In 1919 Bertram Stevens described her as 'the most prolific writer of verse in the Commonwealth'.

Mary E. Fullerton (1868–1946) wrote the classic *Bark House Days* about her childhood in Gippsland. She lived in England in the later part of her life, corresponding regularly with her friend, Miles Franklin.

Barbara Giles (1912–) migrated from Britain in 1923 and began publishing poetry in the 1960s. She has also written for children.

Mary Gilmore (1865–1962) spent her youth engaged in radical nationalist causes, including William Lane's 'New Australia' colony in Paraguay. She edited the Women's Page of the *Sydney Worker* from 1908 to 1931, but accepted the imperial honour, Dame of the British Empire in 1937. She was the 'grande dame' of Australian poetry in the decades before her death.

Helen Haenke (1916–1978) published two books of verse. The second, *Prophets and Honour*, appeared posthumously.

Susan Hampton (1949–) gained a reputation as a poet in the 1970s and has recently begun writing prose pieces. She co-edited *The Penguin Book of Australian Women Poets* with Kate Llewellyn.

Lesbia Harford (1891–1927) graduated in Law from the University of Melbourne, but devoted herself to the labour movement, despite her precarious health. Her poems and a previously unpublished novel, *The Invaluable Mystery*, have recently been published.

J.S. Harry (1939–) has recently published *The Life on Water and the Life Beneath*, which should establish her reputation as one of the leading poets of her generation.

Gwen Harwood (1920–) grew up in Brisbane and moved to Tasmania after her marriage. A gifted musician, she has written librettos for Larry Sitsky. Now recognised as one of the foremost Australian poets, she has won many prizes, including the Grace Leven and the Patrick White awards.

Dorothy Hewett (1923–) has written plays, novels and an autobiography, as well as poetry. She was a member of the Communist Party from the late 1940s to the 1960s, and her plays were among the first in Australia to experiment with non-naturalistic styles.

Fidelia Hill (1790-1854) came to South Australia from England in the first years of settlement. Her book, *Poems and Recollections of the Past* (1840), may have been the first book of verse by a woman to be published in Australia. She died in Launceston, Tasmania.

Nancy Keesing (1923–1993) was an editor for Angus & Robertson in the 1950s and 1960s (for a time, with Nan McDonald and Rosemary Dobson). She edited anthologies of bush ballads and songs with Douglas Stewart, and wrote a study of Australian women's language, *Lily on A Dustbin*. She gave to the nation the Keesing Studio in Paris, which allows young Australian writers to have a period of residence overseas.

Antigone Kefala (1935–)was born in Romania, and came to Australia after the Second World War by way of Greece and New Zealand. She has written a children's book and a novella about her experiences of migration.

Honora Frances Kelly (1848-1898) lived her entire life on Stoney Creek Station in the New England district of New South Wales, 'never once leaving the area', as her family put it. Her descendants published her poems in 1965.

Jean Kent (1951–) works as a psychologist. She shared the National Library poetry prize with John Foulcher in 1988, and won both the Anne Elder and Mary Gilmore awards for *Verandahs* in 1990.

Jeri Kroll (1946–) came to Adelaide from New York in 1978. She has worked as a radio producer, community-arts worker and academic.

Louisa Lawson (1848–1920), the mother of Henry Lawson, published and edited the *Dawn* newspaper for women from 1888–1905, to support women's suffrage and rights. She contributed her own poetry, journalism and stories.

Caroline Leakey (1827-1881) is best known for her novel about an innocent convict woman, *The Broad Arrow*. Born in England, she spent five years in Tasmania (1848-53) and used this experience as material for her novels and poetry.

Kate Llewellyn (1940–) has published both poetry and prose. Her accounts of her life in the Blue Mountains, *The Waterlily*, *Dear You* and *The Mountain* have been very popular. She co-edited *The Penguin Book of Australian Women Poets* with Susan Hampton.

Sumner Locke (1881–1917) wrote the 'Mum Dawson' books, which provided a kind of feminine answer to Steele Rudd's 'Dad and Dave' stories. She also wrote plays. She died after giving birth to her son, the playwright and novelist, Sumner Locke Elliot, and her poems were published posthumously.

Nan McDonald (1921–1974) worked as an editor (with Nancy Keesing, Rosemary Dobson and Douglas Stewart) at Angus & Robertson during its heyday—the immediate postwar years.

Rhyll McMaster (1947–) has published five books of poetry. Brought up in Brisbane, she lived for some time on a farm near Braidwood, NSW, and now lives in Sydney.

Dorothea Mackellar (1885–1968) was a popular poet, her poem 'My Country' (which she wrote at the age of nineteen) being learnt by heart by generations of Australians. The daughter of a wealthy doctor, she lived most of her life in Sydney.

Jennifer Maiden (1949–) has published more than ten books of poetry, and has been awarded several prizes, including the New South Wales Premier's prize for *Winter Baby*. She teaches creative writing.

Catherine Martin (1848–1937) also published as Mrs Alick McLeod. A self-educated intellectual, she was best known for her novels, including *The Incredible Journey* and *An Australian Girl*.

Vera Newsom (1912–) has worked as a teacher and literary reviewer. She has been a prolific publisher of poetry in recent years.

Oodgeroo of the Noonuccal tribe (1920–1993), formerly known as Kath Walker, was a prominent Aboriginal poet and activist, who could claim some credit for the successful 1967 referendum to grant Australian citizenship to Aborigines.

Jan Owen (1940–) lives in Adelaide and has published three books of poetry. Her first book, *Boy With a Telescope*, won both the Anne Elder and Mary Gilmore awards.

Nettie Palmer (1885–1967) was a prominent literary essayist and critic. With her husband, Vance Palmer, she kept up a network of support for Australian writers across the country. She published only two books of poetry.

Charmaine Papertalk-Green (1963–) has worked in Aboriginal research and administration.

Menie Parkes (1839–1915) [Clarinda Sarah Parkes], was the eldest daughter of Henry Parkes, who is often credited with fathering Australian Federation. Henry arranged for the publication of Menie's single book of poems. A.W. Martin has edited *Letters from Menie: Sir Henry Parkes and His Daughter*.

'Sydney Partrige' (Kate Margaret Stone) (1872–1953) wrote short stories and novels as well as poetry, publishing in the *Bulletin* and the *Australasian*. With her husband, she managed the Wayside Press and edited several magazines.

Grace Perry (1927–1987), a paediatrician, was the editor of *Poetry Australia* for more than twenty years, and did much to support the work of other Australian poets and writers.

Marie E. J. Pitt (1869–1948) was a feminist, active socialist and trade unionist. From 1919, she lived with the poet Bernard O'Dowd in defiance of religious and social convention.

Dorothy Porter (1954–) has published novels for children as well as a range of poetry. Her most recent book, *The Monkey's Mask*, is a lesbian detective story in verse.

Wendy Poussard (1943–) began writing poetry when taking part in the women's anti-nuclear demonstration at Pine Gap in 1984. She works in an international women's development agency.

Jean Logan Ranken published five books of poetry during the 1910s. In 1936 she jointly edited a collaborative crime novel, *Murder Pie*, for Angus & Robertson.

Jennifer Rankin (1941–1979) was part of the Sydney 'push' of the 1960s, which was based at the University of Sydney. She published widely before her early death from cancer.

Vicki Raymond (1949–) grew up in Tasmania, but has lived in London since 1981. In 1986 she won the British Airways Commonwealth Poetry Prize.

Mary Richmond seems to have lived in New Zealand as well as Australia around the turn of the century. *Poems*, a collection of her work, was published in 1903.

'Rickety Kate' (Minnie Agnes Filson) (1898–1971) became paralysed a few years after the birth of her son. Unable to move her limbs, she dictated verse to her mother and other relatives.

Elizabeth Riddell (1910–) came to Australia from New Zealand to work as a journalist in Sydney. She has continued to write literary reviews and journalism.

Judith Rodgriguez (1936–) has also published as Judith Green. She is a poetry editor, academic and linocut artist.

Gig Ryan (1956–) has lived in Sydney and Melbourne. Some of her poetry has been written as lyrics for rock music.

Tracy Ryan (1964–) lives in Perth. *Killing Delilah* is her first book of poetry.

Dipti Savaranamuttu (1960–) has worked as a journalist, scriptwriter and academic. In 1989 she was awarded the Arthur Macquarie Travelling Scholarship.

Margaret Scott (1934–)was born in England, and, until recently, taught English at the University of Tasmania in Hobart.

Jemal Sharah (1969–), a diplomat, was born in Canberra to a family of mixed Lebanese and Irish background. *The Path of Ghosts* is her first book of poetry.

Judy Small (1953–) is known as a country-and-western singer and song-writer. She insists that 'From the Lambing to the Wool' and 'Mothers, Daughters, Wives' should be sung.

Edith Speers (1949–) was born in Canada, and came to Australia in 1974. She now lives on a farm in Tasmania.

Jennifer Strauss (1933–) teaches English at Monash University, Melbourne. She is the editor of *The Oxford Book of Australian Love Poems*.

Bobbi Sykes (1945–) was one of the first Aborigines to complete a university education, going on to gain a PhD in education from Harvard. She is a political activist and writer.

Glen Tomasetti (1929–) writes and sings her own songs. She has published two novels, *Thoroughly Decent People* and *Man of Letters*.

Daisy Utemorrah (1922–1993) adapted Aboriginal myths and stories for children. Her book of poems *Do Not Go Around the Edges* was also written for children.

Vicki Viidikas (1948–) was one of the few women accepted as part of the Generation of 1968 group of poets. She has written prose and prose-poems as well as poetry, and has travelled extensively in India.

Ania Walwicz (1951–) was born in Poland, and has made the migrant voice an integral part of her poetry. Her work is best when heard in her own idiosyncratic performance.

Deb Westbury (1954–) lives near Wollongong and is also a sculptor. Her latest book of poetry is *Our Houses are Full of Smoke*.

'Anna Wickham' (Edith Hepburn) (1884–1947) was born in Britain and lived most of her adult life in London, where she was part of literary society. She lived in Australia between the ages of eleven and twenty, and her pseudonym honours Wickham Terrace, Brisbane, where she promised her father she would become a poet.

Judith Wright (1915–) is one of Australia's best-known poets. Born to a New England pioneering family, she has written histories, stories and literary criticism as well as poetry. In the 1960s she became involved in the conservation movement, and in past decades has been active in support of Aboriginal rights.

Fay Zwicky (1933–) was a concert pianist before beginning a career as a university teacher of English. She has written short stories as well as poetry, and now lives in Perth.

ACKNOWLEDGMENTS

We wish to thank the copyright holders for permission to reproduce the following material:

Susan Afterman: 'Grandmother' and 'Soldier Boy' from *Rain*, University of Queensland Press, St Lucia, 1987. **Ethel Anderson**: 'Squatter's Luck' and 'Sleeping Soldier' from *Squatter's Luck and Other Bucolic Eclogues*, Melbourne University Press, Carlton, 1942 [second edition 1954]. **Robyn Archer**: 'The Menstruation Blues' from *The Robyn Archer Songbook*, McPhee Gribble, Melbourne, 1980. **Dorothy Auchterlonie**: 'A Problem of Language' from *The Dolphin*, Australian National University Press, Canberra, 1967. **'Australie' (Emily Manning)**: 'From the Clyde to Braidwood' and 'Two Beaches—Manly' from *The Balance of Pain and Other Poems*, George Bell and Sons, London, 1877. **Judith Beveridge**: 'Fox in a Tree Stump', 'The Lyre Birds' and 'Hannibal on the Alps' from *The Domesticity of Giraffes*, Black Lightning Press, Wentworth Falls, 1987. **Lily Brett**: 'The Excrement Cart' and 'Poland' from *Poland and Other Poems*, Scribe, Brunswick, 1987. **Pamela Brown**: 'Summer Icebox' from *New & Selected Poems*, Wild & Woolley, Glebe, 1990; 'Shaky Days' from *This World/This Place*, University of Queensland Press, St Lucia, 1994. **Joanne Burns**: 'genetics' and 'lung lexicon' from *blowing bubbles in the 7th lane*, Fab Press, Sydney, 1988; 'conviction: a transcript' from *On a Clear Day*, University of Queensland Press, St Lucia, 1992. **Caroline Caddy**: 'Frank' from *Letters from the North*, Fremantle Arts Centre Press, Fremantle, 1985; 'Foreign Aid' from *Conquistadors*, Penguin, Ringwood, 1991. **Ada Cambridge**: 'The Physical Conscience', 'A Wife's Protest', 'London' and 'Ordained' from *Unspoken Thoughts*, first published by Kegan Paul, Trench & Co., London, 1887, reprinted by English Department, Uni College, UNSW-ADFA, 1988. **Caroline Carleton**: 'Song of Australia' from *Song of Australia*, Adelaide [185?]; 'Wild Flowers of Australia' from *South Australian Lyrics by Mrs C.J. Carleton*, J.H. Lewis Platts, Adelaide, [18?]. **Lee Cataldi**: 'the dressing shed', '*kuukuu kardiya* and the women who live on the ground' and 'your body' from *The Women Who Live on the Ground: Poems 1978–1988*, Penguin, Ringwood, 1990. **Nancy Cato**: 'River Scene' from *The Darkened Window*, Edwards and Shaw for the Lyre Bird Writers, Sydney, 1950; 'The Lovers' and 'Mallee Farmer' from *The Dancing Bough*, Angus & Robertson, Sydney, 1957. **Alison Clark**: '*Incipit Vita Nova* (Again)' and 'Reclaiming the Feminine' from *Ananke*, Scripsi, Melbourne, 1987. **Elsie Cole**: 'Indictment' from *Children of Joy*, Lothian, Melbourne, 1928. **Alison Croggon**: 'Songs of a Quiet Woman' and 'Lindy' from *This is the Stone* by Alison Croggon/*Pharaohs Returning* by Fiona Perry, Penguin, Ringwood, 1991. **Zora Cross**: 'Love Sonnet XVII' and 'Night Ride' from *Songs of Love and Life*, Angus & Robertson, Sydney, 1917; 'Sonnets of Motherhood' from *The Lilt of Life*, Angus & Robertson, Sydney, 1918. **Sarah Day**: 'Table Laid for One' from *A Hunger to be Less Serious*, Angus

& Robertson, North Ryde, 1987; 'Kissing the Bubble' and 'Plenary' from *A Madder Dance*, Penguin, Ringwood, 1991. **Dulcie Deamer**: 'Messalina' and 'The Young Martyr' from *Messalina*, Frank C. Johnson, Sydney, 1932. **Margaret Diesendorf**: 'the grey man', 'To break my solitude' and 'Only the gods can hear . . .' from *Holding the Golden Apple: Love Poems*, Phoenix Publications, Brisbane, 1991. **Rosemary Dobson**: 'In a Cafe', 'The Bystander', 'Child with a Cockatoo', 'Cock Crow', 'The Three Fates', 'Visiting' from 'Daily and Living' and 'Who?' *Collected Poems*, Collins/Angus & Robertson, North Ryde, 1991. **Dorothy Drain**: 'Christmas, they say' from the *Australian Women's Weekly*, 29 December 1954. **Eliza Hamilton Dunlop**: 'The Aboriginal Mother (from Myall's Creek)' from *The Aboriginal Mother and Other Poems*, Mulini Press, Canberra, 1981. **Anne Elder**: 'At Haworth' from *For the Record*, The Hawthorn Press, Melbourne, 1972; 'School Cadets' and 'The Bachelor' from *Crazy Woman*, Angus & Robertson, Sydney, 1978. **Diane Fahey**: 'The Pool' from *Metamorphoses* by Diane Fahey, Dangaroo Press, Sydney, 1988; 'The Chinese Astronomer' and 'Dressmaker' from *Turning the Hourglass*, Dangaroo Press, Sydney, 1990. **Mary Finnin**: 'Overtones on Australia Day', 'The Farm Near Norman's Lane' and 'Winter Upland' from *The Shield of Place*, Angus & Robertson, Sydney, 1957. **Mary Hannay Foott**: 'Where the Pelican Builds' and 'In the Land of Dreams' from *Where the Pelican Builds*, Gordon and Gotch, Brisbane, 1885. **Mabel Forrest**: 'The Circus Lion', 'Chaperones' and 'The Other Side' from *Alpha Centauri*, Thomas C. Lothian, Melbourne, 1909; 'Kassaptu' from *Poems*, Cornstalk, Sydney, 1927. **Mary E. Fullerton**: 'Crows', 'Vandal' and 'War Time' from *The Breaking Furrow*, Sydney J. Endacott, Melbourne, 1921; 'Comet', 'Body' and 'Passivity' from *Moles Do So Little With Their Privacy*, Angus & Robertson, Sydney, 1942. **Barbara Giles**: 'Reading an Erotic Novel at a Late Age' from *The Hag in the Mirror*, Pariah Press, Kew, 1989; 'A Careful Childhood' and 'Mama's Little Girl' from *A Savage Coast*, Hale & Iremonger, Sydney, 1993. **Mary Gilmore**: 'The Hunter of the Black', 'Aboriginal Themes' and 'Never Admit the Pain' from *Selected Verse*, Angus & Robertson, Sydney, 1948; 'Nationality', 'The Lesser Grail' and 'Fourteen Men' from *Fourteen Men*, Angus & Robertson, Sydney, 1954. **Charmaine Papertalk-Green**: 'Wanna be White' from *Inside Black Australia: An Anthology of Aboriginal Poetry*, edited by Kevin Gilbert, Penguin, Ringwood, 1988. **Helen Haenke**: 'Motel Dining-Room' from *The Good Company*, The Hawthorn Press, Melbourne, 1977; 'Pear Tree' from *Prophets and Honour: Poems by Helen Haenke*, The Hawthorn Press, Melbourne, 1979. **Susan Hampton**: 'Inside the Skyscrapers', 'Ode to the Car Radio' and 'Stockton' from *Costumes*, Transit Poetry in assoc. with Wild & Woolley, Chippendale, 1981. **Lesbia Harford**: 'I can't feel the sunshine', 'Periodicity', 'Street Scene—Little Lonsdale St' and 'Pat wasn't Pat last night at all' from *The Poems of Lesbia Harford*, edited by Drusilla Modjeska and Marjorie Pizer, Sirius, North Ryde, 1985. **Gwen Harwood**: 'Ebb-Tide', 'Carnal Knowledge I', 'Carnal Knowledge II', 'Father and Child', 'Return of the Native', 'Mother Who Gave Me Life' and 'Bone Scan' from *Selected Poems*, Collins/Angus & Robertson, North Ryde, 1990. **J.S. Harry**: 'eyes' and '"the baby, with the bath-water, thrown out"' from *Hold, for a Little While and Turn Gently*, Island Press, Sydney, 1979; 'a shot of war' from *A Dandelion for Van Gogh*, Island Press, Sydney, 1985; 'The Life on Water and the Life Beneath: 2' and 'Chorus & Protagonists' from *The Life on Water and the Life Beneath*. **Dorothy Hewett**: 'In Moncur Street', 'Anniversary', 'Madame Bovary' and 'Miss Hewett's Shenanigans' from *Selected Poems*, Fremantle Arts Centre Press, South Fremantle, 1991; 'To the Glory of God & of Gwendoline' from *Greenhouse*, Big Smoke Books, Sydney, 1979; 'Owl' from *Peninsula*, Fremantle Arts Centre Press, 1994. **Fidelia Hill**: 'Recollections' from *Poems and Recollections of the Past*, Sydney, 1840. **Honora Frances Kelly**: '"King Jimmy" (Colonial Idyll of the King)' from *Stoney Creek: the Collected Works of Honora Frances Kelly 1848–1898*, New Century Press, Sydney, 1965. **Nancy Keesing**: 'Cicada Song' from *Showground Sketchbook and Other Poems*, Angus & Robertson, Sydney, 1968; 'Detective Story' from *Imminent Summer*, Edwards & Shaw for the Lyre Bird Writers, Sydney, 1951. **Antigone Kefala**: 'The Promised Land', 'Sunday Visit' and 'Barbecue' from *Absence: New and Selected Poems*, Hale & Iremonger, Sydney, 1992. **Jean Kent**: 'After Illness, Grace Notes' from *Verandahs*, Hale & Iremonger, Sydney, 1990; 'Clerical Assistant' from *Practising Breathing*, Hale & Iremonger, Sydney, 1991. **Jeri Kroll**: 'The Towers of Silence' from *Indian Movies*, Hyland House, Melbourne, 1984. **Louisa Lawson**: 'Coming Home' and 'A Pound a Mile' from *The Lonely Crossing*, Dawn Office, Sydney, 1904. **Caroline Leakey**: 'The Prisoners' Hospital, Van Diemen's Land' from *Lyra Australis*, Bickers and Bush, London, 1854. **Kate Llewellyn**: 'Peri's Farm' from *Honey*, Hudson, Hawthorn, 1988. **Sumner Locke**: 'The Left Behinds' from *In Memoriam*, Sydney J. Endacott, Melbourne, 1921. **Dorothea Mackellar**: 'My Country' from *The Poems of Dorothea Mackellar*, Rigby, Adelaide, 1971. Copyright C.K.M. Dredge and B.K. Elkins. **Jennifer Maiden**: 'Space Invaders' and 'In the Gloaming' from *The Trust*, Black Lightning Press, Wentworth Falls, 1988; 'Turning the Bulls Around' from *Acoustic Shadow*, Penguin, Ringwood, 1993. **Nan McDonald**: 'The Lonely Fire', 'The Mountain Road: Crete, 1941', 'Sleep' and 'The Hawk' from *Selected Poems*, Angus & Robertson, Sydney, 1969. **Rhyll McMaster**: 'Profiles of my Father' from *Washing the Money*, Angus & Robertson, North Ryde, 1986; 'My Mother and I Become Victims of a Stroke' from *On My Empty Feet*, William Heinemann, Port Melbourne, 1993. **Catherine Martin**: 'By the Blue Lake of Mount Gambier' from *The Explorers and Other Poems*, George Robertson, Melbourne, 1874. **Vera Newsom**: 'Midnight Snow' from *Midnight Snow*, Hale & Iremonger, Sydney, 1988. **Oodgeroo of the Noonuccal tribe (formerly Kath Walker)**: 'Daisy Bindi', 'Gifts', 'Then and Now', 'Dawn Wail for the Dead', 'Last of His Tribe' and 'No More Boomerang' from *My People: A Kath Walker Collection*, The Jacaranda Press, Milton, 1981. **Jan Owen**: 'This Marriage' from *Night Rainbows*, William Heinemann, Port Melbourne, 1994. **Menie Parkes**: 'Our Darling's Lover' from *Poems*, printed for private circulation, F. Cunningham, Sydney [18?]. **Nettie Palmer**: 'The Mountain Gully' and 'The Barrack Yard' from *Shadowy Paths*, Euston Press, London, 1915, reprinted in *Nettie Palmer*, edited by Vivian Smith, University of Queensland Press, St Lucia, 1988. Copyright the Estate of E.V. and J.G. Palmer. **'Sydney Partrige' (Kate Margaret Stone)**: 'Sund'y' and 'Capitalism' from *The Lie and Other Lines*, The Koolinda Press, Adelaide, 1913. **Grace Perry**: 'The page will not

contain you' from *Snow in Summer*, South Head Press, Berrima, 1980;
'Leaving the House' from *Journal of a Surgeon's Wife*, South Head Press,
Sydney [?]. **Marie E.J. Pitt**: 'Reveille', 'The Clan Call' and 'The Reiver'
from *The Horses of the Hills*, Lothian, Melbourne, 1911; 'Autumn in
Tasmania' from *The Poems of Marie E.J. Pitt*, Edward A. Vidler, Melbourne,
1925; 'Australia's Tommy Atkins' and others reprinted in Colleen Burke,
Doherty's Corner: The Life and Work of Poet Marie E. J. Pitt, Sirius, North
Ryde. Copyright William Pitt and Lionel Chatham Pitt. **Dorothy Porter**:
'Wunjo' and 'P.M.T.' from *Driving Too Fast*, University of Queensland
Press, St Lucia, 1989; 'Nefertiti Rides Me' from *Akhenaten*, University of
Queensland Press, St Lucia, 1992; 'Money for Nothing' and 'How Poems
Start' from *The Monkey's Mask*, Hyland House, South Melbourne, 1994.
Wendy Poussard: 'Boston Tea Party' from *Outbreak of Peace: Poems and
Notes from Pine Gap*, Billabong Press, East St Kilda, 1984. **Jean Logan
Ranken**: 'The First Night in Sydney Harbour' from *Dream Horses and
Other Verses*, Australasian Authors' Agency, Melbourne, 1912. **Jennifer
Rankin**: 'Forever the Snake', 'Song', 'Love Affair 36' and 'Old Currawong'
from *Collected Poems*, University of Queensland Press, St Lucia, 1990.
Vicki Raymond: 'Static', 'Laundromat', 'An Episode of the Class Struggle',
'Open Day, Highgate Cemetery', 'Chat Show' and 'Night Piece (Freycinet
Peninsula)' from *Small Arm Practice*, William Heinemann, Richmond,
1989. **Mary Richmond**: 'Sydney Harbour' from *Poems*, Elkin Mathews,
London, 1903. **'Rickety Kate' (Minnie Anges Filson)**: 'To the Main
Roads Board' from *Rhymes & Whimsies*, Lawson & Bray, Sydney, [193?];
'Before Kosciusko' from *Bralgah: A Legend*, Jindyworobak Publications,
Adelaide [194?]. **Elizabeth Riddell**: 'News of a Baby', 'Here Lies', 'The
Time of Life' and 'To Stay Alive' from *From the Midnight Courtyard*,
Angus & Robertson, North Ryde, 1989. **Judith Rodriguez**: 'Five Poems
on Memory', 'Mudcrab at Gambaro's' and 'Family' from *The House By
Water: New and Selected Poems*, University of Queensland Press, St Lucia,
1988. **Gig Ryan**: 'Breaking and Entering' and 'Not Like a Wife' from *The
Division of Anger*, Transit, Glebe, 1980; 'Disinformation' and 'Poem' from
Excavation, Pan/ Picador Books, 1990. **Tracy Ryan**: 'Killing Delilah' and
'City Girl' from *Killing Delilah*, Fremantle Arts Centre Press, South
Fremantle, 1994. **Dipti Savaranamuttu**: 'Sealing the Deal' and 'Like Yeast
in Bread' from *The Language of Icons*, Angus & Robertson, Pymble, 1993.
Margaret Scott: 'Housework', 'Proteus' and 'A Walk on the Beach' from
The Black Swans, Angus & Robertson, 1988. **Jemal Sharah**: 'Black Swans
in St James's Park' and 'Pastoral' from *Path of Ghosts: Poems 1986–93*,
William Heinemann, Port Melbourne, 1994. **Judy Small**: 'From the Lamb-
ing to the Wool' and 'Mothers, Daughters, Wives' from *The Judy Small
Songbook*, Orlando Press, Rozelle, 1986. **Edith Speers**: 'Confessional' from
By Way of a Vessel, Twelvetrees Publishing, Sandy Bay, 1986. **Jennifer
Strauss**: 'Report from the Mid-Century Mark' and 'The Snapshot Album
of the Innocent Tourist' from *Labour Ward*, Pariah Press, Kew, 1988; 'A
Mother's Day Letter: Not for Posting' from *Voices* vol. 2, no. iv, National
Library of Australia. **Bobbi Sykes**: 'Monopoly', 'Fallin'', 'One Day' and
'Black Woman' from *Love Poems and Other Revolutionary Actions*, Uni-
versity of Queensland Press, St Lucia, 1989. **Glen Tomasetti**: 'Don't Be
Too Polite, Girls!' from *Songs From a Seat in the Carriage*, R.A. Hulme and

M.G. Dugan, Heidelberg West [197?]. **Daisy Utemorrah:** 'Our Mother Land' and 'Black Man' from *Do Not Go Around the Edges*, Magabala Books, Broome, 1990. **Vicki Viidikas:** 'The Country as an Answer' and 'Going Down. With No Permanence' from *Condition Red*, University of Queensland Press, St Lucia, 1973. **Ania Walwicz:** 'The Fountain' and 'The Abattoir' from *Travel/Writing* by Phillip Hammial and Ania Walwicz, Angus & Robertson, North Ryde, 1989. **Deb Westbury:** 'Self Portrait in a Mirror' and 'Albatross Road' from *Mouth to Mouth*, Five Islands Press, Wollongong, 1990. **'Anna Wickham' (Edith Hepburn):** 'Divorce' and 'The Marriage' from *The Writings of Anna Wickham, Free Woman and Poet*, edited and introduced by R.D. Smith, Virago Press, London, 1984. Copyright James and George Hepburn. **Judith Wright:** 'Woman to Man', 'At Cooloolah', 'Request to a Year', 'To Another Housewife', 'Australia 1970' and 'Wedding Photograph, 1913' from *A Human Pattern: Selected Poems*, Collins/Angus & Robertson, North Ryde, 1990; 'For a Pastoral Family' from *Phantom Dwelling*, Angus & Robertson, North Ryde, 1985. **Fay Zwicky:** 'Isaac Babel's Fiddle Reaches the Indian Ocean', 'Summer Pogrom', 'Chicken', 'Tiananmen Square June 4, 1989' and 'Soup and Jelly' from *Poems 1970–1992*, University of Queensland Press, St Lucia, 1993.

INDEX OF FIRST LINES

INDEX OF POETS AND TITLES